IN PRAISE OF GH

"Ginanne Brownell is up to something wonderful. Her book on ghetto kids in Kenya producing beautiful classical music has all the right elements for an incredibly moving story that will appeal to lots of people. The Kenyan slums are such rich repositories of all the good and bad in the world. The poverty is as depressing as anywhere on Earth, but so many people in these places do shockingly kind things for each other. I'm always moved by the spirit and warmth, and a book set here is not glorifying poverty but understanding it. Her book lifts spirits and makes us feel connected to others in a way that few stories do. Ginanne's language is crisp, decisive, fun, and authentic."

— Jeffrey Gettleman, Pulitzer Prize winning author of *Love, Africa* and global correspondent for *The New York Times*

"Ginanne Brownell's book is an inspiration, a hope, a voyage into a way we can make the world a better place. Using classical music as a vehicle for life change, she shows us how music is a way of altering children's lives—from misery and poverty to beauty, to empowerment, to radical change. This is surely a book for our times, as a vision of how we can spark impetus and make the world better for the next generations."

— Janine di Giovanni, award-winning journalist and author of *The Vanishing: The Twilight of Christianity in the Middle East*

"Ginanne Brownell has written a riveting account of this group that is so much more than an orchestra. She shares the good times when music and community have triumphed, and also the challenges encountered over the last decade, writing unflinchingly of the lows

as well as the highs. Theirs is a phenomenal story and this is an important and insightful record of it."
— **Lucinda Englehart, Nairobi-based award-winning film producer**

"For nearly twenty years, I've followed Ginanne Brownell's forays into foreign cultures with huge interest. Every time she leaps on a plane and delves into the society she studies on arriving there, she finds fascinating, complex scenarios. Particularly at a time of roiling unease and political hand-wringing in the West, the story of how classical music can transform the lives of poor Kenyans is a much-needed window on hope, grit and change."
— **Carla Power, two-time Pulitzer finalist and author of *If the Oceans Were Ink* and *Home, Land, Security***

"*Ghetto Classics* is a vivid, haunting portrait of a community's strength and resilience in the face of daunting challenges. Ginanne Brownell brings a nuanced, insightful eye to the stories of the children and adults for whom music is both a refuge and a source of hope. While Nairobi's biggest garbage dump is dirty and dangerous, Brownell's encounters with those living beside it, and making their livings from it, are deeply affecting—and ultimately inspiring."
— **Beth Gardiner, journalist and author of *Choked: Life and Breath in the Age of Air Pollution***

ghetto classics

How a youth orchestra changed a Nairobi slum

To Elizabeth —

best wishes —

Graham Broadbent

Readers are encouraged to go to www.MissionPointPress.com to contact the author or to find information on how to buy this book in bulk at a discounted rate.

Published by Mission Point Press
2554 Chandler Rd.
Traverse City, MI 49696
(231) 421-9513
www.MissionPointPress.com

Design by Sarah Meiers
Cover photo copyright © Mia Collis

ISBN 978-1-958363-50-8
Library of Congress Control Number 9781958363508

Printed in the United States of America

ghetto classics

How a youth orchestra changed a Nairobi slum

Ginanne Brownell

MISSION POINT PRESS

In memory of my dearest Paps, who taught me that education is everything.

Foreword

It was just another hectic day in August 2016 when I got the call. I was running around between meetings in one part of Nairobi and then over to Korogocho, the slum in the northeastern part of the city where I run my youth orchestra, Ghetto Classics (GC), to deal with an administrative issue. By the time I picked up my then three-year-old daughter from a playdate in yet another part of the Kenyan capital, my phone was at one percent. As I wove through Nairobi's notoriously clogged traffic on my way finally back home, my phone started buzzing with a British phone number. I picked up and Ginanne Brownell introduced herself, saying she was a London-based American journalist. She said she wanted to write a story about my work with classical music in Kenya and [with] GC. "I am writing the piece for *The New York Times*...," she said, and then the phone battery went dead.

Over the years I have encountered a number of journalists who were keen to cover what we were doing in Korogocho, and so for me, it was just another interview that she wanted to set up. But in the few days she spent with me in September 2016—she attended the first ever concert we did for GC parents and also sat in on music lessons—I could see she was not only interested in my story of forming the orchestra, but she was also taken with the kids and the program. I noticed she really engaged with them and I could tell she had not only a good reporter's instinct, but she was a person who really cared about what she was writing.

A few weeks later, in fact the day after her *New York Times* piece ran, we had a fire at St. John's, the community center, church, and school where GC is based. It was an extremely upsetting and challenging experience for us on a number of different levels. Ginanne happened to coincidentally reach out to me that evening, and after me commiserating with her about the fire, she told me why she was calling. Her visit with us had had a profound impact on her. She had decided that instead of writing a general book on girls' education that she had been working on during her trip to Kenya, she was interested in writing some kind of book about Ghetto Classics that would encompass a number of themes and topics: from education and development to arts, culture, and community empowerment.

From our initial conversations in Nairobi—we spent a lot of time in my car as I shuttled her from meeting to meeting with me—I knew that all these topics were of great personal interest to her. I had been very happy with how *The New York Times* piece had turned out: it was accurate, and I think very much portrayed our goals and achievements. After she gave me her full rehearsed pitch, I didn't hesitate to say, "Yes!" We both agreed that what made sense was to do a biography of Ghetto Classics, as we were coming up to the tenth anniversary of its founding. (In the end, the book actually covers from our beginnings through to the Covid pandemic and right up to the cusp of our fifteenth anniversary that we will mark in 2023.)

I figured a book like this could not only serve as an archive for the orchestra, it would also remind us of what we have done right over the years and also where there was room for improvement. She was given carte blanche on this book because I wanted to have it be a warts and all biography so that everyone—from myself to my team and our supporters—could learn from what she saw and found. Having Ginanne be an outsider to not only the community, but Kenya as a whole, I think also gave her a level of distance where she could really focus in on a viewpoint without layers of bias and personal filters.

Ginanne, who I can say has truly become a friend over the last six-plus years, came out to see us a half a dozen times to do reporting, research, and writing. I introduced her to a few GC students who I thought helped capture the story of what we were trying to do, but also separately she met and struck up friendships with other GC members. I remember thinking that she had an ease with my students and tutors, where they warmed up to her, and both interviewer and interviewee benefited from the conversations. She was conscientious in her reporting. And she also understood the nuances of writing about disadvantaged slum kids that was not done in a condescending way, but one in which she knew gave them the power to tell the story from their own narrative.

She would often check with me—we joke to this day that she is my stalker—to make sure I was okay with how things were progressing on the book. If there was something that was slightly awkward or delicate, we talked over how she should best cover it. (Within our GC community there are some harrowing personal stories that are highly sensitive, involving abuse, rape, exploitation, violence, and addiction.) A few times she went with some of my students and staff into the slum to speak with locals and also walk through the large garbage dump that abuts St. John's. It is an experience not for the fainthearted, and she was keen to tell the stories not only of the people who came from there that were in my orchestra, but also to better understand the gradations and complexities of what life is like in a place like Korogocho. As well as visiting us in situ, she also went to see two of our students, Teddy Otieno and Stephen Kamau Maina, one summer in East Hampton, New York, where they were participating in a classical music summer camp. A few years later, right before Covid, Ginanne also met us in Lausanne, Switzerland, when I brought a handful of GC members for a concert with members of the local conservatoire.

This book has proven a great way to reflect on our program—on our successes and also our challenges—and it will serve to be a guide as we go forward into our next decade. To me it has proved insightful in that it has given me a keen understanding into how the outside world views the work that we do. I also have gotten a chance to get to hear the voices of our members, which is sometimes wholly different than conversations I have with them. I think it was easier for them to talk about their experiences with someone who has some distance from the day-to-day operations of the program. It's been fun, it's been frustrating, but overall, I am so happy to have our story out there in the wider world.

Elizabeth Njoroge
Executive director and founder, Art of Music Foundation

Introduction

Every May, the dry Kenyan savannah greedily gulps up the rains that push through and head up over the Rift Valley, dumping small oceans across the lands. They wipe clean the rust-red dirt that clings to the branches of banana and acacia trees dotted across the Ngong hills. These rains drown the streets of Nairobi with water and millions of one-inch *kumbikumbi* (flying termites) seemingly come out of nowhere, similar to a plague of locusts. The sound of their transparent, tan-hued wings flapping in a hysterical death flutter on the ground reverberates as loudly as the rumbling distant thunder. They soon perish, piled up in puddles, their wings cracking as people dismissively trudge over them.

That was why Simon Kariuki Ndungu (Simon K.) told me to bring my boots.

I'd been coming to Nairobi for almost three years following the story of Ghetto Classics (GC), and while I had on many occasions from the grounds of St. John's Community Church—where the orchestra was headquartered—stared into the steaming, fetid hundred-acre abyss of the Dandora and Ngomongo dump sites, I had never set a flip-flopped foot inside them. But over time it felt neglectful and even wimpy on my part to have never ventured in to see for myself what countless GC kids—past and present—had to endure scrounging to make paltry earnings or get scraps for a meal. The rains in May 2019 had made the dump sites soggier and buggier than usual and so Simon K. warned me of this when I asked him to take me into Dandora. (It would be insanely dangerous and inherently stupid to go in unaccompanied.) "You will need to wear boots and not open shoes…it's too mardy [*sic*] when it rains," Simon K. wrote me on WhatsApp, an epically long conversation string that had been ongoing since we had first met in September 2016. "I talked to gangs at the dumping site, they want $20 for the tour. It's because they are my friends. They normally charge $200."

I was getting something of a family and friends discount because over the years, Simon K., who was the day-to-day manager of Ghetto Classics at St. John's as well as well-respected across the Korogocho community, had also become my friend, as had a number of GC members, like violinists Emily Onyango and Martha Aluoch Awura and tuba player Kevin Obara, as well as Elizabeth Njoroge, the founder of GC. Now whenever I arrived at St. John's to see GC rehearsals, I would be greeted with huge smiles, warm hugs, and always from cellist Stephen Kamau Maina, but known more simply as just Kamau, a concentrated wide-eyed look of bemused surprise. The *mzungu kichaa* (loosely translated as "crazy white person"), which was how I jokingly referred to myself, was back again with more questions and lame wisecracks.

It was never anything I had expected would happen when I first went to the Nairobi slum of Korogocho in September 2016 to write a piece for *The New York Times* about Elizabeth and GC.[1] I'd viewed it like any other assignment, though this had a slightly precarious twist of me having to go deep into an oftentimes turbulent slum to listen for the strains of classical music. I had seen poverty before, of course, but I had had the chance to contemplate very much about how people living in slums actually survived; I just had a vague notion that life was tough and likely quite hopeless. While in many cases this is true, there is also a contagious vibrancy and aspiration within many of the people who live there, which is something I quickly came to understand during my first visit.

The first day I went into Korogocho with Elizabeth, I was aghast by what I saw. But I tried hard to put on my practiced, objective, and world-weary journalist face as we drove past mangy puppies eating vile comingled detritus strewn on the potholed dirt roads, and large bloodied chunks of meat—often headless skinned goats—covered in flies hanging on hooks in front of ramshackle wooden kiosks. Wrinkled women, some effervescent, some bleak, who were likely

---

1 Most locals, including those who live in Korogocho and the surrounding neighborhoods, refer to it as a slum, versus the more politically correct development term of "informal settlement." In keeping with the local vernacular, throughout the book I therefore refer to Korogocho and other informal disadvantaged areas as slums.

much younger than their faces portrayed, sold recycled junk from the dump, hanging their secondhand wares of irons, electric tea kettles, and keyboards from strings along the road. Meanwhile, burly, seemingly brusque men in dirty, sweat-soaked T-shirts were heaving and pulling *mikokoteni* (wooden carts) filled up with yellow plastic jerrycans or firewood. I looked over at Elizabeth to take her temperature of the situation and she seemed calm, so I tried to act like this was all completely natural to me.

Just as the guard was opening the turquoise gates so we could be driven into the St. John's compound that included a school, church, community center, and library, Elizabeth pointed out GC member Teddy Otieno, who, along with his musical colleague Kamau, had just come back from spending part of the school break at a music camp in East Hampton, New York. "Teddy, how you doing today, eh?" she asked as he was walking through the gates. He looked down and then glanced sideways at her, mumbling that he was okay. "Great, well, remember to keep teaching the stuff you learned in New York," she said brightly, as the driver pulled into the courtyard and parked. Though we had just met a few hours earlier, Elizabeth and I had bonded pretty quickly, and she confessed that she was worried that Teddy, whose twin brother, Lamek, was also in the orchestra as a violinist, had found the transition back to his reality tough.

Elizabeth said he had been a bit mopey and there seemed to be some anger underneath as well, something she had never seen from him before. "I am worried and I want to talk to his parents," she said as we got out of the car.

As I made a note to have a chat with Teddy about his experiences in the US, we were engulfed by kids, some in holey burgundy and green school sweaters while others were turned out in crisp white shirts, running up to the car, excitedly shouting, "*Mzungu, mzungu*" (white person), both at me and to each other, cracking up as they did. They threw up their hands for me to give them high fives and then a few of them rushed over to Elizabeth to excitedly tell her things in a mixture of Swahili and English. While she multitasked between listening to the kids and speaking with Simon K., who I was hurriedly introduced to, I had a chance to survey the area around the football and basketball pitch and a number of the small buildings.

I noticed that there seemed to be a lot of dust getting kicked up from the soccer balls that many of the kids were playing with around on the pitch, which was enclosed by a chain link fence that had gaping holes and was generally falling apart. At first, I thought the haze that was engulfing Teddy as he headed towards the community center to get his tuba out of the locker was from the dirt pitch.

But then I noticed there was a choking sulfur smell to it and realized it wasn't the dust that was causing everything around to take on a bronzish-grey fogging patina. It was the smoke blowing swiftly from the dump that encroached almost up to St. John's rusty, chocolate, corrugated walls. Long-beaked grey hadada ibis birds cawed a vociferous disconcerting tune in flight overhead, and my stomach started to churn from the stench of the smoke, rotten food, and chemicals billowing from the gorge of waste. The thought that people had to live next to the dump left me with a gnawing empty feeling in my gut, and I thought to myself that this might be the least likely place on the planet where classical music had found itself a home.

Over the course of the weekend, and later with follow-up calls to Simon K. and a few others like music advisor Levi Wataka—who made up what I later dubbed the "GC ecosystem"—I was increasingly awestruck with what Elizabeth and her musicians had accomplished since GC's founding in 2008. On the edge of this slum of slums, where waste from all over the city, including from other informal settlements, was dumped on a daily basis, something truly beautiful had been planted and was flowering. But it would be inherently naïve to say that it took an outsider like Elizabeth to introduce these qualities of hope and potential to Korogocho—it was there all along. It just needed the right synergy to grow and flourish.

* * *

The reason I had even come to Nairobi was because I had a layover from Tanzania, where I had spent two weeks doing research on a potential book about the barriers that girls faced when it came to their secondary education.

As a freelance journalist, I always looked for stories I could spin off from my travels and since I had recently been writing a lot about classical music, I was intrigued to see what was happening in that genre in the Kenyan capital. I even tried to multitask at St. John's by interviewing a few of the GC girls when I was there on my first day, asking some of the young teens to describe their walks to school nearby the dumps and how oftentimes it was tricky for them to continue their education due to their economic and societal circumstances.

While I was enthused about the subject of girls' education, it just wasn't flowing, as I had no cohesive theme and an almost paralyzing case of writer's block about what I wanted to say. When I got back to London, I found I was also struggling with my story on Elizabeth, but in a different way because I had over-reported the piece (meaning I had too much good stuff not to use) and I was finding it hard to whittle it down to just 1,200 words because I was still so struck and touched from the trip. Ghetto Classics had all the elements of things that got me fired up: education, music, development, empowerment of girls and young women (and men), and the role that the arts can play in helping communities flourish. And yet I couldn't touch on many of these themes in a short, pithy story that was supposed to be written with a light touch.

I did finally file my piece, but for weeks after my thoughts kept returning to Korogocho. I was haunted and enticed by the place and the people.

I wondered how the gentle Simon Mungai was doing on his trombone and how his mother, who had been so proud of him, was aching from her mornings working in the dump. I pondered if Teddy had finally adjusted to being home again. I had met and briefly interviewed Martha Aluoch as she had put her violin away in her case, and she had told me she wanted to be a journalist, so I pontificated on how realistic this dream was, given her lack of access to opportunities. I was curious about why conductor and percussionist Brian Kepher had seemed to steer me away from talking with his mother. And I had been struck by Kamau's jovial and cheeky mom, who had so wonderfully expressed that after she dropped her son off at the airport, she kept looking up into the ink-bottle blue night sky, wondering which plane overhead was winging her son to America.

So I decided to call Elizabeth to say that I wanted to change gears and instead write about Ghetto Classics, and asked her what she thought. "Well, it could serve as a wonderful archive for us," she chuckled, obviously having no idea where this journey was going to take us. "So, okay, sure, let's do this." I asked when I could come back to do more reporting. "February," she said after thinking for a few seconds. And so it began.

One

Dressed in her Sunday best, Margaret Wambui walked with purpose through the rubbish-strewn dirt alleyways of Nairobi's Korogocho slum on a scorching Sunday in September 2016. She nodded at neighbors she knew and looked beyond people she imagined might be trouble. As she entered through the gates of St. John's Primary School and Community Center, she didn't pause to look at the washed-out mural of Jesus walking on water. Nor did she pay any attention to the hand-painted mission statement next to it on the wall stating that the school provides education especially for "the orphans, the recovering street children, and the very poor." Margaret moved along past the two-story beige-painted library and a number of smaller buildings used as classrooms, heading straight through to the rundown open-air cement amphitheater with more fading biblical murals and its panorama of the massive garbage dump site just over the walls. She sat down heavily, sighed, and wiped at her sweaty face. She was the first person in the audience.

This was also the first time she would be seeing her sixteen-year-old son, Simon Mungai Wambui (Simon M.), play his trombone in concert, a show that had been set up especially for the parents and families of members of the Ghetto Classics youth orchestra who practiced there every Sunday at St. John's. Margaret had a fierce determination to get the best seat in the house. "He is very talented," she said proudly in Swahili, with her son translating. "It feels incredible to be here for this."

Life had never been easy for Margaret. She rarely spoke of her childhood, to the point that Simon M. knew next to nothing about his grandparents or if he had aunts and uncles. Margaret wasn't even sure how old she was—something somewhat common in Kenyan slums, where many births go undocumented. But Simon M. figured she was in her early fifties.

Margaret had five children but was estranged from two of them. Her husband, Daniel, had been a village elder in Korogocho, a job that was so stressful that he developed a pack-a-day smoking habit. In 2011, after a long battle with throat cancer—including losing his voice and having to use an electrolarynx to speak—he died. His death meant that not only did she and Simon M., at that point the only child still living at home, have to move to a smaller corrugated shanty, they had also lost much of their income. They were solely dependent on Margaret's money from scavenging in the dump. Ever since Simon M. could remember, his mother has gotten up before sunrise from Monday to Saturday and headed into the dangerous and toxic Dandora dump site, where she would hunt for plastic, glass, and metals to sell for recycling. She had no other options. To this day it is Nairobi's largest landfill, though it was supposed to have been closed down in 2002. But that never happened.

Not only was scavenging a filthy job that put her health at risk, as 850 tons of everything from hospital and chemical garbage to household, airline, slaughterhouse, and restaurant waste was dropped off every day, but it was dangerous too. The site was run by criminal gangs who, ironically, referred to their job as the dump's security. These gangs, who often armed themselves with guns and knives, and might be high on drugs, glue, or buzzing from alcohol, for years held murderous turf wars within the dump. Simon K. said they hid their weapons amidst the rancid waste where pigs, goats, rats, cows, and people also hunted for scraps. The waste that people like Margaret collected was then sold by the kilo for about fifteen Kenyan shillings (KSH). (This amounts to fifteen cents.) And most days Margaret was able to scavenge about twenty kilos. It was backbreaking, dirty, dangerous work, all for less than three dollars a day. And that was on a good day.

* * *

This whole concert had been her son's idea. Tall and long-limbed with a glowing, warm smile, bright, earnest eyes, and a humble but positive demeanor, Simon M. was a good, sensitive boy. He had joined Ghetto Classics over two years before, on February 2, 2014. "I remember that day," he said with a beaming smile, "because for me it was like a second birthday." Simon M. had gone to primary school at St. John's. Around the time he was about to sit for his secondary school entrance exams, he learned from a friend about the GC music program that took place on weekends at St. John's. "I was relaxing on a Sunday after church and was hearing some music coming from one of the buildings, and I thought, 'What is this?' and I was afraid," he remembered, adding that the sounds of the instruments and the style of music was completely foreign to him. "I was amazed when I saw the instruments and I was especially excited when I saw the trombone. I got interested in it because I liked the funny look of it." He then heard a blast of its notes. "It is a very mighty instrument with that deep voice." This crystalized to him that the trombone was going to figure prominently in his future.

Two and a half years after joining GC, practicing almost every day, learning how to read music, and performing in a number of classical music concerts across the Kenyan capital, Simon M. had an idea. Elizabeth Njoroge, the founder of GC, who was a pharmacist by training and a classical music lover her whole adult life, asked the orchestra after a concert what the teenagers and young adults would like to do next. As other members started throwing out their suggestions, Simon M. said, "We should have a concert for our parents." He explained that he thought it would be a good chance to not only have their parents hear and see what they were up to every Sunday, they could also meet Elizabeth. It would also be a great opportunity for her to meet many of them. The vast majority of GC members' parents had never been exposed to classical and jazz music before. Many, like Margaret, were fans of gospel music or other genres like hip-hop or R & B. They had no clue what their kids' instruments looked like, let alone the sounds their kids could make emanate from them.

Close to the stage on that sunny Sunday, Margaret sat bold and upright, as thick smoke from the dump curled above her in the sky. The smell fell over the audience just as the brass section, which included Simon M. and tuba player Teddy, took deep breaths. The woodwind players, including clarinetists Tracy Akinyi Ogutu and Celine Akumu, pursed their lips. Meanwhile, the string performers, like violinists Emily Onyango and Martha Aluoch Awura, gripped their bows. Brian Kepher, the twenty-one-year-old percussionist and part-time conductor of Ghetto Classics, then dramatically lifted his baton. He gave a slight nod towards the percussion section, where Charity Akinyi was at the ready with her drumsticks. Kepher, as he is more commonly known, then cued the teenagers to begin. The GC musicians—some wore jeans and T-shirts with the Ghetto Classics logo, "Making Music Makes a Difference," emblazoned across the front while others, like cellist Kamau, wore soccer warm-ups and flip-flops—performed works that included Pachelbel's "Canon in D" and Hans Zimmer's "Pirates of the Caribbean."

As large black and white marabou storks swooped in and out of the hills of garbage, their wings making a discomfiting deep baritone "whoop-whoop" noise as they launched themselves into the sky, the uplifting musical notes bounced off the cement walls. Half notes and quarter notes cheerily floated up towards the dump on one side and across towards the slum on the other. As the last bit of "Hapo Zamani"—by South Africa's Miriam Makeba—echoed through the amphitheater, the audience of over 270 people yelled and clapped loudly. One middle-aged man, the whites of his eyes a malarial yellow, cheered and stamped his feet as his soiled khaki trousers drooped past his waist. He stunk of *chang'aa,* a homemade alcoholic brew sold in the slum. A few kids looked at him nervously—possibly his children—mortified by his dancing, slurring, and stumbling. Margaret, her face rarely conveying much emotion, gave a delighted smile towards the stage.

Just before cake and juice were put out for the audience by Simon K., a former gang member, and Kevin Obara, who grew up in a home where his mother brewed *chang'aa* and who was now charged with keeping track of all the instruments, Elizabeth bounded onto the stage to thank the families for coming. With her thousand-watt smile and an enthusiasm that was infectious, she encouraged parents to keep sending their kids each week so that they could continue to learn and have fun. What she did not have to say was something that many of the plugged-in parents understood implicitly. Ghetto Classics was not just about teaching their children how to read and play music, it was also a tool for educational, developmental, and social change in the slum. And the parents also knew that for a few hours every weekend, their kids were removed from the dangerous pitfalls of poverty.

* * *

Four months after the parents' concert, Simon M. and his mom had to move to a new home because she was concerned for their safety. Since the violent 2007 presidential election where over 1,200 people were killed and 350,000 citizens were displaced across Kenya, there were ongoing ethnic tensions in the slum between the Kikuyu, Luo, and other ethnic groups. Simon M.'s family members were Kikuyu, and the fact that his father had been a village elder had exacerbated strains for his relatives. And while this was always at the back of his mind, on one hot day in February 2017, Simon M. was in a good mood. Partly it was because school was out for a week-long break. That meant that Simon M. could spend a good portion of the day practicing his beloved trombone.

As he and his friend Emily Onyango, a violinist with GC, waited for a handful of scruffy grey goats to cross a small metal bridge that led to his new home, they talked about how his father had made attempts to deal with the insecurities and tensions in Korogocho and the neighboring slums. "The thugs were not happy because it was their way of life to make sure things were insecure, so they couldn't tolerate what my father was doing," he said matter-of-factly. "So, they started conflict between our families and others, and it was very dangerous. When he passed away, we were left without anything and we were forced to move."

As they crossed the unstable bridge that passed over a polluted small creek choked with blue plastic bags and other bits of trash,

Simon M. and Emily discussed the boundaries between Korogocho, Lucky Summer, and Kajiji, the neighborhood where Simon M. and his mom now lived. The bridge, dubbed Rape Bridge because of the number of sexual assault incidents that had happened nearby, for years had been a turbulent crossroads where a number of people from the various informal communities commuted to the Dandora dump for work (next to St. John's was the equally toxic—and illegal—Ngomongo dump site—see appendix two for further details). However, like so many things in the slum, people just got on with their lives, understanding the dangers but not deterred in doing things that had to be done, from paying for their food to earning money for their kids' school fees. To the naked eye, there wasn't much to differentiate between the various neighborhoods. They were all populated with a mixture of corrugated shanty dwellings, tuck shops—which sold everything from cigarettes to phone cards—and vegetable stands, barber shops, and used tire kiosks that hawked petrol in clear glass bottles.

But for those who lived in the slums, it was obvious where one area ended and another began. This new neighborhood was somewhat safer than Korogocho, and as he and Emily rounded the bend towards his home, a toddler girl in a soiled pink party dress reached out for his hand and smiled. Almost directly across from the alleyway from his home was the Boma Rescue Center, a daily drop-in center for street children. Emily waved and shouted greetings in Sheng, a slang mixture of Swahili and English, to a few kids. As a teenager, she had spent a year there when tensions had become untenable with her stepfather, and she sometimes went back to visit and volunteer.

Since school was out and he did not have to walk the one kilometer to his secondary school, Simon M. had all the time in the world to practice his music. In the living area of his mother's clean but dark home, his sheet music sat loosely on a wooden chair. "This," he said, "is my mama's house." Now that he was a teenage boy, it was customary to live in a separate place from his mother. Even if his father were still alive, he would have had to sleep somewhere else. His smaller room was a few doors down. "Mom still makes food for me," he said, touching at his face. "The only thing is, I am not supposed to sleep here; so the whole day I can be here, but at night I have to move." As he sat down on a brown sofa and Margaret quietly settled in another chair against the wall, a few young women outside chattered away, washing dishes using a communal water tap. A toddler girl in a burgundy dress kept peeping through the hanging curtain that served as a barrier between the doorway and outside, letting in glimpses of the midday sunlight.

Just as a baby chick ran into the house and quickly back out again, Simon M., dressed in a pressed white and brown plaid short-sleeve button-down shirt, explained why he viewed the day he joined Ghetto Classics as his second birthday. "After I completed my exams for secondary school, I had no hopes of continuing my education since my mother could not afford to pay for my school fees," he said. He added that he thanked God every day—he is Catholic—that Elizabeth had given him hope and encouragement and helped him get a spot at Our Lady of Fatima, a local secondary school. "When I came to GC," he added, "I thought, 'Whoa, the whole world has changed now.'"

GC had become a salvation for his education. Like many of the children who participated in the program and who were considered to be at risk of dropping out of school, Simon M. got his school fees paid for via donations to the Art of Music Foundation. The not-for-profit foundation was the umbrella organization that Elizabeth formed in 2009 that included Ghetto Classics and the Kenya National Youth Orchestra (KNYO). While technically goverment-run primary and secondary schools are free in Kenya, there are peripheral costs like books, school uniforms, and oftentimes even a rental fee that has to be paid for school desks. Elizabeth, who seemed to have a homing device to know when kids were in trouble, also sometimes gave children a bit of cash to buy food if their parents had not made enough money that week to buy much.

Simon M., who said his favorite classical music piece was Tchaikovsky's "1812 Overture," was shy about accepting handouts. When other kids eagerly took treats or food, he often said "no" out of pride and principle. But he did accept money for his school fees because he understood how important his education was for himself and his family. One day he hoped to make enough money to care for Margaret. He did not want to end up like his siblings. His older brothers worked manual labor jobs in and around Korogocho. One was a construction worker who built houses, while the other operated a forklift in the dump. The sister Simon M. was still in touch with, who lived in the coastal city of Mombasa, worked as an agent for M-Pesa—"M" for mobile, and "pesa," which means "money" in Swahili. M-Pesa is a mobile phone-based money transfer, financing, and microfinancing service run by Safaricom, the largest mobile provider in East Africa. But he saw that his sister really still struggled to make ends meet.

Simon M. was at the top of his class in secondary school, in part because he was motivated by the fact that he was lucky to even be there. During term time, he was out of the door by 6:00 a.m.—with a bit of breakfast if there was any food left over from dinner the night before—and at school by 7:00 a.m. "Secondary school is very intense," he said, smiling and looking over at his mother, whose short greying hair was mostly covered in a white-and-pink striped woolen knit hat. "I am a day student, but you have to compete with the boarding kids who have a long time to study, so we have to be more concentrated." After dismissal at 5:00 p.m., he would then grab his books. Walking quickly over to St. John's, Simon M. would get thirty minutes of trombone practice in before the gates were locked with a thick padlock for the night at 6:00 p.m. And after church on Sundays, he studied for a few hours before heading to St. John's for GC tutorials and orchestra practice.

Ghetto Classics was divided into different groupings. There was Orchestra A (of which Simon M. was a member), which was made up of those who had the highest level of musicianship. Then there was Orchestra B, filled with mostly younger kids who had recently started playing instruments. Orchestra C included both children and some young adults—GC did not have an age limit for joining—who were new to the program, and just learning how to read music and play on recorders. By 2021 an estimated thousand-plus kids from Korogocho had passed through the GC program at St. John's. Meanwhile, another 950 children in other disadvantaged areas around Nairobi and Mombasa had also learned music through Link Up, a

Carnegie Hall music initiative run by the Art of Music Foundation. (While officially called the Orchestra of Schools Initiative, it's most often referred to as just simply Link Up Kenya.) There were also over three hundred kids in the Ghetto Classics Mukuru Kwa Ruben orchestra—another informal settlement in the northwestern part of the city—that launched in 2018, some of whom had previously participated in Link Up.

Simon M. described his daily life when school was in session. "It is a busy week full of music and education," he said. He had big goals in life and wanted to be both a professional musician and some sort of scientist after completing university studies. He had also recently been introduced, through Elizabeth's connections, to a mentor who taught IT at Nairobi's Kenyatta University. The two met every few months to play squash, browse in bookstores, and have coffee.

Margaret, who up to this point had been sitting quietly in the corner playing with her skirt, chimed in to say she had always supported Simon M.'s dreams. But she admitted that at first, she was concerned it was not realistic to take time away from his studies to focus on music. "Comparing him to other kids in the community," Margaret said, "he is going in the right direction." At that first concert four months earlier, Margaret had been absolutely thrilled to see her son play. She could not believe that he knew how to follow all the notes. During much of the performance, though, she worried that Simon was going to get tired because the trombone is both a long and physical instrument. But she also came to realize not only how talented her son was, but also how important the program had been for him. She was also especially pleased because she had a chance to see not only positive role models among his peers, but also that he had been given access to a world that she could never in a million suns provide for him. "Sometimes when I am running late for practice," he said with a chortle, "she now chases me out of the house yelling at me to get moving."

Grabbing his rucksack filled with sheet music and books, Simon M. said goodbye to Margaret, who was about to head off to buy fruit at the local market. As he and Emily walked towards St. John's, they discussed how as a parent, Margaret was something of a rarity in that she was very involved and kept a tight watch on Simon M.'s activities. Margaret had taken great interest and pride in her son's accomplishments, especially when it came to his school grades and music. Many parents in Korogocho were so focused on day-to-day family survival that they did not have time to follow up on what their kids were up to when not in school. And with so much free time on their hands, it was easy for kids to slip into the dangerous traps of growing up in a slum. That included everything from being involved in criminal gangs to drug and alcohol addiction, teen pregnancy, and prostitution. "Music is safe," said Emily, as a boda-boda driver whizzed past on his moped. (For a small fee, these unlicensed drivers ferried people across the slum but were also sometimes involved in crimes like muggings, bag snatchings, and rape. It was also a dangerous job, as years later Simon K. and I saw a dead boda-boda driver, blood streaming from his head, his face covered by a thin piece of cloth, lying on the side of the road after being knocked off his motorbike presumably by a passing truck.)

"I sacrificed myself to music, but everything I got was fantastic," Simon M. said with a beaming grin, happy to have a whole day to practice on his beloved trombone. What Simon M. did not know at the time was that his devotion to Ghetto Classics later proved to be a lifeline for Margaret and his survival.

Two

As Elizabeth sank down into a plush chair at a poolside table at the Muthaiga Country Club, she ordered a big glass of cold white wine.

It had been a long, exhausting September Friday in 2016. She'd spent the morning ferrying back and forth across the Kenyan capital, running GC errands. She then had had a long working lunch at a café in one of the many malls dotted across Nairobi. In the afternoon, she'd headed to St. John's so she could see how things were coming together for the parents' concert that was set for the upcoming Sunday afternoon. Though Korogocho—with its streets that smelled of rotting food and piss, and the chaos of goats, dogs, drug dealers, boda-bodas, chirpy schoolchildren, and industrious adults all jockeying for space—and the posh country club—with its appealing bright salmon-colored stucco buildings next to a shimmering aqua swimming pool, manicured lawns, and quiet, pleasant walkways canopied by massive yellow-trunked acacia trees and flowering magenta hibiscus bushes—were only a few miles apart, they were proverbial worlds away from each other.

For some, this aesthetic juxtaposition could be difficult to acclimatize to after being in the bowels of Korogocho all day. But Elizabeth transitioned easily back into her upper-middle-class Kenyan life.

As Elizabeth wiped away some of the Korogocho dust from her square wire-rimmed glasses, her sister, Irene Mukiri, a lawyer dressed in a smart, cream business suit, and their friend Jaine Mwai, in crisp tennis whites and carrying a racquet bag, arrived poolside with laughter and kisses. As her sister and friend sat down and ordered drinks and snacks, they all noticed that the governor of Nairobi County (essentially the mayor of the capital), Evans Kidero, a big, strapping bespectacled politician, was sitting two tables away. "Hey, how are you?" Elizabeth shouted towards him, getting up quickly to greet him as he lumbered over to their table. They easily conversed, and joked about how they were both guiltily lulling away the early evening even though they each had so many things to do.

"So, I was just over at Korogocho with this journalist for *The New York Times,* and it was really smoky today, eh," she said, watching as Evans's politician's grin quickly faded when he realized Elizabeth was going to demand, again, action on getting the illegal Ngomongo dump closed. "It's just really hard for my kids to practice when they are breathing in the polluted smoke and chemicals, you know," she said, smiling at Evans, but with a look that made him realize this was not going to be the relaxing and convivial conversation he hoped to have.

"Well, we need to talk about it," he said, grasping her hand in a way that suggested the conversation was over. He kissed Irene and Jaine, and then made a quick dash back to his table where his friend sat, enthusiastically waving to the women.

"He just ran away, didn't he?" Elizabeth asked rhetorically with a cheeky smirk on her face, her glass of wine sweating with condensation, and the flame of the citronella candle bouncing its light off her glass. Irene joked that even when she was socializing in her down time, Elizabeth was always championing for her Ghetto Classics kids.

Elizabeth had always been something of a bleeding heart. Born in 1971 and raised on a coffee farm near Nairobi with her three siblings, she had grown up in a life of privilege, the daughter of a high-ranking civil servant, David, and a homemaker, Beatrice. At the age of four, Elizabeth started taking piano lessons and quickly fell in love with music. As a teenager, she attended a well-respected government-run academic high school where students came from across Kenya, and she had been a music prefect. "I was from Nairobi, from a relatively well-off family, but there were kids from other places who had never used a toilet," she said as she sipped her wine. One year, before the school term started, her mother bought her two lovely sweaters to take back with her to school. When the weather got cooler, Elizabeth noticed that one of her less fortunate classmates didn't have anything to keep warm, so she gave the girl one of her sweaters. "My mother came to school and noticed another girl wearing it and I said to her, 'But she did not have a sweater, and I had two, so she can have my sweater,'" she said. "And to this day she has never forgotten that story."

Elizabeth—or Liz to her friends—got involved with her school's Christian Union and would often do volunteer projects to help the needy. But she still also loved music, having continued with her piano lessons, and she even began experimenting with songwriting. Her parents encouraged her interest in music—until it came time to do her A-levels. "I always remember where we were, in the car by Jamhuri High School in Nairobi," she recalled. "My father asked me what I wanted to do with my life and I said, 'I don't know, but I would like to work with children, and I would like it to have something to do with music.' And then he asked me again, 'What would you like to do?' so I knew that was not the answer he was looking for. That was when he said no more music lessons. It was very hard."

So, instead, she focused on her studies and did well enough to gain a place in the biochemistry department at Canada's McMaster University in Hamilton, Ontario. But by her second year at the university, that call of music was too strong for her to ignore. Elizabeth joined the university choir, where, with her first proper exposure to classical music, she fell in love with the genre and was encouraged to take voice lessons focused on more operatic and classical music. Previous to that, she had been more of an R & B fan. In her last year in Canada, she took a classical music course that further piqued her interest in the genre. Her voice teacher encouraged her to study music, but Elizabeth had also been accepted to pharmacy school at Scotland's University of Strathclyde, something that led to what she joked was her "existential crisis."

Arriving in blustery Glasgow that autumn of 1994, Elizabeth popped into the Royal Scottish Academy of Music (now renamed as the Royal Conservatoire of Scotland) and picked up a glossy prospectus. For an entire week, she seriously flirted with the idea of going there instead to study music, but in the end, she said she just didn't have the guts. However, throughout her three years in Glasgow, she took music lessons, and joined the university chorus and the Royal Scottish National Orchestra choir. After graduation, she moved to London for a year's work experience and sang with the London Symphony Orchestra, and then moved across southeast England to work in various locales as a pharmacist. But her teenage dream of combining kids and music still loomed in the back of her mind.

In 2002, Elizabeth went back to Kenya for a sabbatical; it had been thirteen years since she had moved away, and while she loved living abroad, "I felt like I was building someone else's country." Mwai Kibaki had just been elected president, ending the long-standing dominance of the Kenya African National Union party that had governed the country since independence from Britain in 1963. There was a euphoric feeling that permeated across the country, and that time of optimism inspired Elizabeth. So, she made the decision in 2003 to move back to Nairobi and found a stable job as a pharmacist. But she soon realized that the balance she had been able to find—first in Canada and then in the United Kingdom—between music and her professional career was a lot tougher back home. "When I came back to Kenya, I found that classical music belonged to a very small group of people, people who are white in color, and you had to belong," she said with a bemused smile. "To even know which concert was happening you had to have been on the mailing list. At that time, the Nairobi Orchestra had one Black person in it."

Quickly tiring of her job and having that awkward assimilation that many expats feel coming back home after living abroad for so many years, out of a "personal need" she started holding music recitals for friends, often with her friend Duncan Wambugu on piano and herself singing. Elizabeth also got the idea to found a music newsletter that she modeled off of *BBC Music Magazine*, a publication focused on classical music that she had pored over when living in the UK. In her monthly mailing, she would highlight both an international classical musician of the month as well as a Kenyan musician. And, in a plucky and bold move, she spammed it out to hundreds of people across Kenya—many of whom were in positions of power in government, business, and the diplomatic sector—in the hopes of getting advertising dollars for her burgeoning publication. One of those spammed recipients was Michael Joseph, then the CEO of Safaricom, which is partially owned by Vodafone. "Michael," she said, "changed the course of my life."

Having received her email—and being a huge fan of classical music himself—the white South African businessman emailed Elizabeth back, encouraging her to keep sending him her newsletter. The newsletter eventually grew into a proper magazine, with Elizabeth registering her business under the company name Art of Music in 2007. She sent it to Michael, who in turn told his marketing people that he wanted Safaricom to advertise in each magazine edition. "I came to Nairobi from Budapest, where there is a lot of classical music," he reflected. "So, when I went to Kenya, obviously there was so little, so when Liz wanted some help, I said, 'Fine, let's do it.' So that was my introduction to her."

Later on, in 2007 Safaricom started sponsoring a two-hour monthly classical music radio program on Nairobi's Capital FM with Elizabeth as the bubbly and charismatic host. The show proved to be popular with Kenyans from all backgrounds. "I remember there was one guy who called in who said he played my show in his *matatu*," she said, referring to the privately owned minibuses that are ubiquitous across Kenya. "That showed me that all sorts of people loved classical music, and it needs to be on the menu. There are people who absolutely love it and cannot live without it."

This was an especially important realization during the increasingly tense times in Kenya. The December 2007 presidential election saw Mwai Kibaki, a Kikuyu, beat Raila Odinga, a Luo. That set off a chain of violent protests and killings, leading to a political, economic, and humanitarian crisis in the country. It raged until February 2008, when a power sharing agreement was reached with the help of former UN Secretary General Kofi Annan. Meanwhile, Elizabeth understood that music had a way of helping unite people. At this point she was also organizing classical music performances in local Nairobi malls, and even a classical music festival called Classical Fusion, also sponsored by Safaricom. "All the concerts and operas that she organized—and she was a fantastic organizer—she brought [this music] to the Kenyan people," Michael said. "She pushed [to] make it much more accessible. She is a dynamic person, one of those special people."

All this focus on music made it clear to Elizabeth—and those around her—that her days counting out prescription pills were numbered, so in 2008 she quit her pharmacy job in order to focus full time on her Art of Music projects. But since her hobby had now become her job, Elizabeth needed to constantly be on the lookout for advertisers to help fund the magazine. That same year, one of her friends, who was then the CEO of the Moi International Sports Center in Kasarani, in northeast Nairobi (and a stone's throw from Korogocho), invited her to a meeting he was having with an acquaintance from UN Habitat to talk about putting in a basketball and football pitch near the slum of Korogocho. Elizabeth gate-crashed their meeting at a branch of Java Coffee, a popular Kenyan chain, and gave her magazine presentation to the UN representative.

Also in attendance at the meeting was Father John Webootsa, a Kenyan Catholic priest who was there because the sports pitches would be part of his parish jurisdiction. "I told them what I do, and I knew it was not going to work in terms of advertising, but I still sat through the meeting," she remembered. "I gave out my magazines and Father John took my card." Fairly new in his parish position, which encompassed the slum of Korogocho, with St. John's as the parish church run by the Italian-based Comboni Missionaries of the Heart of Jesus, the priest was committed to doing things differently. "What caught my attention was the situation of the youth," Father John recalled in an email, recollecting on those early days. "Many in Korogocho seemed to have lost hope at a very young age, [and] this is because of the poverty in their homes. They never even saw the need to go to school, [and] many of them [took part in] crime, prostitution, and selling drugs, [some] from as young as ten years old."

Father John was keen to help people in the slum, and he was also good at getting international donors to bring in money for projects. Armed with the card Elizabeth had given him, he called her the next day. "He said, 'Why don't you come and teach my kids music?' and, at that point I thought I could do anything, so I said, 'Yeah, no problem,'" she recalled with a laugh. "It was the biggest accident ever."

While Elizabeth had a deep, passionate love for music, she knew little about the pedagogy of teaching it and so instead of winging the lessons, she knew the perfect person to contact—her friend Levi Wataka, a pianist, music teacher, and high school rugby coach. Over the years the two had worked together on recitals across Nairobi and Mombasa, and they had talked endlessly about trying to improve the classical music scene in Kenya. Especially when it came to young people. Though Levi was teaching music at St. Andrew's School, Turi—a posh international school in the Rift Valley, which was five hours away from Nairobi—Elizabeth convinced him to come along and check things out with her. "She is like a magician," Levi said. "She moves her wand and somehow she makes things happen."

When Elizabeth and Levi showed up at St. John's on that first Saturday in May 2008, Father John had rounded up fourteen teenagers who all stood around, curious and skeptical about how exactly this new youth program was going to take shape. One of those in the original cohort was the stocky, cerebral twenty-one-year-old Simon K. He had grown up in the turbulent maze-like alleyways of Korogocho. His father was an alcoholic and his older brothers were criminals—one of whom had been shot and killed by police—which meant that his family had a bad reputation within the community. "From an early age, I was involved in crime—smuggling guns for a gang—but my mother realized this, and she took me back to her village in Nakuru County, which was 170 kilometers away from Nairobi," he said matter-of-factly. Simon K. recalled that after four years away from the illicit temptations of Korogocho, and while living with a religious uncle who always strongly instilled in him the importance of academics, he had become a totally different teenager. When he learned his mother, Monica, was struggling financially and emotionally with her life, Simon K. made the decision to go back to Nairobi in 2001.

Back home in the overcrowded slum, Simon K. found that many of the boys he had grown up with had now become serious hardened criminals. A few tried to lure him back into the dangerous underworld where they existed. (Many of those friends have since been killed in gang violence.) But Simon K.'s years up-country had changed him.

His goal now was to help his mother and to also try to help change the community where there seemed to be little hope for young men like him. This youth music program for neophytes intrigued him. "I remember Liz arrived in a small green car and she had a guitar," he recalled with a deep laugh, averting his eyes as he talked, a nervous habit that he eventually kicked. Simon K. loved singing and was in the church choir, so GC had grabbed his interest, even though by looking around at the other young people who had gathered that day, he knew he was the oldest. He seriously contemplated how this motley bunch were going to be turned into musicians.

On that first day in the classroom after Elizabeth and Levi introduced themselves, they showed the teens a few clapping games to teach some initial concepts of timing, notes, and rhythm. The young people seemed absorbed and were having fun, which inspired Elizabeth. After they left Korogocho later that morning, she asked Levi if he wanted to continue helping her with the music program, which initially was just going to be a choir. He eagerly agreed and even convinced his St. Andrew's School, Turi, colleague Karis Crawford, a Michigan-born violinist and teacher, to help him out each week.

As everyone who was involved in those early days recalled, the music program, which at that point had no formal name, was pretty rough going. They taught music notes on a moveable black chalkboard, with the students sitting behind desks in a half-built community center within the St. John's complex. "Our biggest challenge in the beginning is we had nothing: we had no instruments, we had no books, absolutely nothing but ourselves, so we just had to go in and teach theory," said Karis. "But the kids did not understand what we were doing because they didn't have instruments. They were interested in what we were teaching but they were like, 'What is a scale? I don't understand.'"

Another major hurdle in the early days was that sometimes the kids simply didn't show up for lessons. For Levi and Karis, who had to get up before dawn to drive over from the Rift Valley to Nairobi, that was also very exasperating. "I would text Father John on a Friday and ask if we were on for the next day, and he would say yes," Levi recalled. "And sometimes we would get there and there would be nobody. And I was so angry." After the second time it happened, Levi ran into Simon K. and two of his sisters. When Levi demanded to know why no one had shown up that morning, annoyed that he had wasted his morning driving, Simon K. explained that there had been a water crisis. Most of the kids had spent their morning standing in a never-ending queue for hours to get a chance for their share.

It was not that the kids didn't want to be at the music classes, Simon K. said, but growing up in the slum was all about survival. Music was not a priority when there were life-threatening obstacles they had to deal with. "We are used to you guys coming in and feeling that your time is important, but until you can live in our reality, if we need to get water, we are going to prioritize water," Simon K. told Levi. At that point, Simon K. had never even heard the term "development" before, but he innately understood through his own lived experience many of the concepts, conflicts, and obstacles debated over in the field of aid. "The music is going to have to fit into our lives. So, until you learn that you cannot help us," Simon K. said as Levi calmed down and listened.

Simon K. explained that they had seen so many NGOs come into the slum, claiming that they were going to "change" and "empower" the lives of Korogocho residents by starting a new program—be it art therapy classes, health clinics, or a boxing hall. But once the do-gooders invariably ran out of funding, they would close the program, leaving behind frustrated residents, some of whom had come to depend on the offerings. "So if you are one of those, that's fine, we will smile and take pictures," Simon K. told Levi, "but if that is who you are, you aren't here to stay." Levi was dumbstruck and took to heart what Simon K. had said to him. Levi realized that he needed to teach the music classes without expectation. If they turned up for their classes on Saturday (which later moved to Sunday), that would have to be enough for the time being. Meanwhile, Elizabeth, who had initially viewed the music sessions as a side project to her Art of Music activities, realized this was becoming time consuming and the program needed more attention and focus.

At the end of August 2008, after several months of the young people—including Simon K., Erick Ochieng (who later became

GC's chief conductor), and Samwel Otieno—practicing and learning basic musical concepts, Elizabeth wanted them to show off what they had been learning on their weekends. St. John's was hosting a community festival, and Elizabeth signed up the choir to perform. She also reached out to the Kenya Conservatoire of Music to ask if they would accompany them as they performed "Hallelujah Chorus" from Handel's *Messiah*. That afternoon, there was a crowd of about 750 local residents having a great time enjoying loud live reggae, hip-hop, and benga music being performed in the amphitheater.

Karis changed the mood totally when she took the stage to play a piece from Paganini on her violin, and then the choir took the stage, with Levi conducting. As the choir began to sing, the audience was astonished by the notes that were being sung by their sons, daughters, neighbors, and friends. "We were like aliens," Elizabeth remembered with a giggle. "They looked at us like, 'What the hell?'" But despite the bemused reaction from their community to their singing, the kids stuck it out through to the end and the audience reacted positively. For most of the kids in the choir, their public debut was an acknowledgment that they had done something pleasing and positive. "That was my first experience performing; I was so nervous," Samwel said. "But it was so exciting and so good."

It was a boost for everyone—including Elizabeth. After nailing that performance, she thought the kids needed to be stretched because a number of them were getting more and more serious about their music. They had proved to themselves and their community they could sing well. And that is how the orchestra part of Ghetto Classics developed. "We needed to challenge these kids more, and that is when it became really serious," she said. "But I had no idea how to teach an instrumental program. I am a singer. Where do you get instruments from?"

Around the same time that Elizabeth decided to expand the program that was now officially called Ghetto Classics—a name one of the then GC members, Daniel Onyango, came up with one day sitting under a tree with Simon K. and others. (It was chosen, said Simon K. because it was "easily recognizable and something people could associate with.") Levi decided that since the new school year was coming, it was untenable to keep driving every few weekends down to Nairobi. So he bowed out but stayed on as an unofficial advisor, a role that he still has to this day. In need of both instruments and a teacher, Elizabeth reached out to Atigala Luvai, who was then head of the Kenya Conservatoire of Music. He not only donated a number of battered instruments for the kids to practice on, he also put her in contact with a music teacher.

There was not a lot of money to fund the program. They initially limped along from small donations made by Elizabeth's friends and supporters. That meant that not only could Elizabeth barely pay the teacher (sometimes they could only afford to have lessons every few months), but she also had to pay for a taxi to transport the instruments from the Conservatoire to St. John's. Or sometimes the instruments would be kept in the trunk of Elizabeth's car. And though it was tough traipsing across Nairobi with instruments or trying to find funding to pay for one more weekly lesson, Elizabeth realized that she was finally doing what she said she wanted to do all those years ago when she was driving around with her father—she was working with kids through music. "It was never something I thought I would be doing full time," she confessed. "Everyone thought I was mad—my parents, my friends, my parents' friends, friends I had not spoken to in six years who would say, 'I hear you are doing music.' And I never liked to talk about what I was doing because then I would have to explain, and I just knew it was what I wanted to do and what I felt I should be doing. There is no explanation, so maybe to compensate for it, I worked like a dog."

While she was trying to make a go of GC—writing grant proposals, and giving some tours of St. John's for people who had heard there was a nascent orchestra in the slum on the edge of a garbage dump—she was also still organizing classical music evenings. Plus, she was still putting together the Classical Fusions festival as well as trying to decide what to do with the magazine. It was proving a lot to balance. One evening in the spring of 2009, while sitting with Irene and a friend, Judy Macharia, at the Muthaiga Country Club, she ran into **Julius Kipng'etich**. At the time, he was the CEO of the

Kenyan Wildlife Services (KWS), and he had been responsible for putting their ads in her magazine.

The four of them got talking. Soon another friend of Julius's, a lawyer named Rachel Mbai, who had experience with setting up foundations, joined them. They spoke and debated over what form Elizabeth's organization should take, and what she hoped to do with GC. Trying to run a profit-making business while also trying to run a nonprofit music program was not working. Something had to give. So in the gardens that evening, with the lingering sweet hints of jasmine in the air, they decided that the Art of Music as a for-profit company should be dissolved. In its place, the Art of Music Foundation should be set up.

As they sipped their cocktails and casually mapped out future plans for the foundation and GC—their laughter and conversation bounding animatedly across the ever-green mowed lawns while cicadas chirped their evening pleasantries—just a few miles away was Korogocho. That initial cohort of GC members was spending the evening dodging gangsters. They went to bed on dirt floors in their shanty homes, the smell of smoke from the dump drifting through their nostrils, and the sounds of not-so-far-off gunshots and screams ringing in their ears.

Three

That cacophony of violence had been the soundtrack to Kevin Obara's childhood.

In a place like Korogocho, where death, rape, poverty, violence, substance abuse, and crime were mainstays, Kevin's story was uniquely wretched. Born at home in December 1996, Kevin, though he was known by his friends as just Obara, was the second youngest of twelve children of his mother, Margaret Auma, and his father, Japuonji, a Luo name that Kevin said means "teacher." His youngest sister, Mercy, was born in 1998, on the day the US Embassy was bombed in Nairobi, and, according to Kevin, she was born outside at the Gikomba Market because the shock sound of the bomb "ousted her" from Margaret's womb. Kevin's father had had a good job with Kenyan Railways, and there were even stories, which Kevin only knew through Margaret, of his father travelling to Japan for work and bringing back toys for his youngest son. The family didn't initially live in Korogocho, but in a better area along the Thika Road, and up until Kevin was about three, his childhood had been a happy, if nondescript, one.

But in the time span of just three years—from 1999 to 2002—six of his siblings died. Two of his brothers, Ochieng and Johana (for whatever reason, the son was given a name that traditionally is given to girls), died under mysterious circumstances related to headaches and stomach pains (something Kevin blamed on witchcraft). Then, in a freak accident, Nancy (Mercy was later renamed Nancy in her memory), who had been playing outside the family home, was hit by a piece of tire rim that someone had been rolling on a nearby roof. The little girl died instantly. And two preteen sisters, Akoth and Aketch, were both brutally raped and murdered. A fourth sister had also died,

23

but when asked about her name and the circumstances of her death, Kevin couldn't recall either because he had been so young at the time. Plus, he said, it pained his mother to talk about it too much.

To lose one child would be heartbreaking, but for half of them to die was almost unfathomable, and the pain became too much for his parents to bear.

Kevin vaguely remembered the funerals, the crying, the confusion, the crises. He also recalled that soon enough the harmony and happiness at home was replaced by arguments and acrimony. Even before his mother packed their bags and took her remaining six children away from that pain (only to be later replaced by the difficulties of life in a slum), Japuonji had morphed into someone the family no longer knew. Some neighbors claimed Margaret was cursed, and while those cruel rumors upset her, what hurt Margaret the most was that her husband blamed her for the deaths of their children. "My mom saw the family as a total failure," Kevin said with a hint of bitterness.

Margaret had had little access to education growing up, and she found the only way she could support her family in Korogocho was by making *chang'aa*. At first Margaret just sold it on from suppliers, but she soon realized that brewing it at home could make her that much more money. However, that meant that not only did less-than-savory characters start hanging around the house all day and into the night, but also, over time, that Kevin and his siblings were recruited to help. From the age of ten, Kevin knew all about making *kangara*, the dirt-brown, almost soupy, liquid base that was a mixture of water and jaggery or *sukari nguru*, a thick, porous, molasses-colored block made from sugarcane. (Brewing it had been illegal for many years, but in 2010, in an effort to take business away from brewers who used toxic chemicals like formalin or battery acid to give it more of a kick, under a new Kenyan law *chang'aa* was now supposed to be distributed and sold in glass bottles.)

Boiled in iron drums coated in thick soot, with a bucket sitting on a stool that is kept inside, as it cooks, a vapor is released and water is poured on top to cool the steam, which condenses into a liquid inside the bucket. Regulating the heat is essential so that the *kangara* does not boil over into the bucket. Since it was illegal to brew before 2010, Kevin's family would make it at night (to make four jerricans of *chang'aa* would take until dawn), but sometimes the police, knowing what was going on, would pop in. Often it was just so the family would pay them off with a glass and two hundred Kenyan shillings, because, as Kevin charmingly described, his mother had a "sweet mouth" and could usually talk the *mbang'a* (slang for cops) out of hauling them off to jail. But sometimes Kevin, his mother, and his other siblings would be arrested and kept in lockup for a few nights, mostly so the cops were seen to be making an effort to close down the illegal brew business in the slum.

One of the fundamental rules that most moonshiners will tell you is that you never drink your own product. But Margaret, absolutely off her head from grief, didn't adhere to this tenet and drank ... a lot. She argued that she had to drink it to show customers she trusted her brewing, because any small mistakes during the brewing process could kill someone.

And when she drank, Kevin said it was hell on Earth. He and his mother had massive fights and though she was his mother, he lost a lot of respect for her and spoke back to her, saying nasty things. Luckily a neighbor, seeing the family in turmoil, took Kevin under his wing, counseling the boy that he should not talk to his mother like that. In late 2007, he took Kevin to a rehabilitation facility called Hands of Care and Hope. Run by Catholic nuns, they fed him and began giving him basic education so that when he enrolled in primary school the next year at the age of twelve, he was not too far behind his peers.

However, in 2009, he had to drop out of school for a time because of an incident that took place one balmy evening. Some customers who had been drinking *chang'aa* in Kevin's home witnessed his aunt give Margaret some money to go to the store. Soon after, they followed Margaret outside, but Kevin, busy entertaining one of the church elders, did not pay much mind. "Then we heard yelling and screaming for a few minutes, but I did not know who it was, and then in the third minute, my instinct told me to go out," Kevin remembered. "I had a torch and when I flashed it, the three men ran away. But my mother is tough and she still had the money in her hands." They had stabbed her in four places—the head, the neck, near her heart, and in the arm—and Kevin rushed his mother to a local clinic. However, according to Kevin, in some Nairobi slums these shoddy medical facilities are often run by doctors who have either lost their licenses or have not even completed medical school. The particular doctor who stitched up Margaret gave Kevin some antibiotics to administer to her and told him to take her home. A few days later, Kevin went back to the doctor, who asked him if Margaret had ever woken up. "He had purposely done a bad job doing the stiches because he did not think she was going to make it, and I cursed him, saying, 'You will die from my mother,'" Kevin said. He added that the man had since died, "so karma is real."

Kevin was back in school by 2010, baptized as a Catholic, and sent to St. John's for the rest of his primary education. He then started secondary school in 2012. But by 2013, the family was hard pressed to afford his fees. However, this coincided with the fact that Kevin had heard about Ghetto Classics through his friend Samwel, who had been in GC's first cohort and had since grown into a talented trumpet player. "GC was lifesaving for me," Kevin said in September 2016, during an interview in the practice rooms at St. John's. Though the thin, towering tuba player with a sharp square jawline and sunken cheeks came across as quite shy, he exuded an enchanting smile and was exceptionally polite and charming. "I live in an area that is full of thieves, so to find someone who is my age and not a thief is very hard," he said shyly. "Ghetto Classics secured me from that life, so instead of staying idle, because you know idle hands make the devil's work, my time is here now."

At that time, Kevin was in form four (the last year of secondary schooling in Kenya), and his best classes were English, Kiswahili, and history. A member of both the orchestra and also of a jazz group, the Heritage Band, with Erick Ochieng, Joseph Omondi, and Celine Akumu, his school fees were paid for by the Art of Music Foundation. Elizabeth, he said, was his savior, and she would quietly give him money for food when she thought he looked more gaunt than usual. "I can say she saved my life," he said, a shy smile coming across his lips. "Music relieves me from stress and it boosts my confidence. I think about my music and then I cannot hear what is happening around me."

Four

Even as a teenager, Simon K. inherently understood that music had the power to change people's lives.

In 2005, while still in secondary school, he and three friends from Korogocho founded a singing group called Hope Raisers that had its musical roots not only in reggae and hip-hop, but also in local rap genres, including *genge* and *kapuka*. Their focus was on creating social change through song, in the belief that music could unify people and it could also be used as a driver to stimulate community development. Simon K. and his friends had been inspired in part by a local band, Kalamashaka, who had come out of Dandora singing political music that helped people from the Eastlands slums express their grievances. The group had had mild success outside of Kenya with songs like "Tafsiri Hii."

Hope Raisers released a track called "G8" with the chorus of:

> *G8, we have a question for you.*
> *Why do you want us to suffer?*
> *Why do you want us to perish?*
> *We are the creditors.*
> *Cancel debt, cancel debt.*
> *You the G8*

Released on YouTube and MySpace, a thinner, younger version of Simon K., dressed in a white tank top, silver necklace, and sunglasses, rapped and gesticulated with his hands in the video. Hope Raisers got a bit of traction, both within Korogocho and across Nairobi, for melodically articulating through a beat issues that affected people's everyday lives. (There had even been some talk with a

German contact that maybe Hope Raisers could perform their song with Bono at the G8 summit in Germany in 2007, but that never came to fruition.) The dump, the drugs, the death, the violence, and the lack of opportunities had been musical motivators for Simon K. and his bandmates. Hope Raisers wanted to empower their friends and community, and they used music in a positive way to vent their angers and frustrations.

Simon K. has always been something of an enigmatic character, constantly dropping random facts of his life with very little braggadocio: as a ten-year-old, he knew how to stealthily hide guns in the dump and in the alleyways of Korogocho, but he had also been, years later, an invited speaker at the International Teaching Artist Collaborative (ITAC) music education conference at Carnegie Hall in New York City.

Coming from the background that he did, Simon K. knew only too well the pitfalls of poverty. As a kid he had scavenged in the dump, and he hated seeing his peers and their younger siblings having to depend on other people's waste for survival and to feel like there was nothing positive that would ever happen in their lives. He was always quick to point out to anyone who would listen that life in the slum was not hopeless. And that while growing up in a place like Korogocho definitely had its hardships, it was also a place with a strong sense of community and many role models with deep moral convictions who would try to guide those who were going astray. Two of those who Simon K. was drawn to were Father John and Japeth Olouch Ogola, a community activist and social worker who had spent a good portion of his life living and working in Korogocho. They helped instill in him a desire to volunteer within and empower the community. "I did it to keep myself busy," he said, "because I was seriously stressed [out] at that age."

After he graduated from high school in 2007, Simon K. found a job doing construction work around St. John's, and, in his spare time, he sang in the church choir, worked on music with his bandmates, and continued volunteering. (Hope Raisers also started a roller skating club that Simon K. helped coordinate until a bad injury to his arm put him out of commission.) He also started a small business selling waste from the dump, including used airplane pillowcases, to make money. Part of those funds went to help fund Hope Raisers's music and community activities.

When Father John mentioned to Simon K. in May 2008 that a woman, Elizabeth, was going to start a weekend youth choir at St. John's, he was dubious but curiosity got the better of him. Elizabeth intrigued him, partly because he could easily see she, a middle-class Kikuyu who had been educated abroad, was out of her element in a place like Korogocho. The contemplative, goateed young man equally intrigued Elizabeth, who saw that Simon K. was passionate about bettering his community. While Simon K. liked the conceit of what GC was trying to do, he did not have high hopes for how things were going to progress, in part because of Elizabeth's outsider status. "I realized pretty quickly that Elizabeth did not really understand the politics of the community, and she did not understand how things go around here," Simon K. recalled. Almost right from the start, he volunteered himself to get things going because he felt that how the program was being run was not sustainable.

The first thing Simon K. felt needed to be sorted out was convincing naysayers that Korogocho needed GC as much as GC needed them. So, he went out and started talking to people and garnering goodwill. He also had to convince young people that while GC did have some funds, it was not a program of handouts. "There was," Elizabeth said, "a lot of suspicion of what we were doing." If young people wanted to learn music and have something fun to do on weekend afternoons, great, but if they thought it was anything more, they would be sorely mistaken. Having Simon K. massage that process was integral to GC's early survival. "I was and am the face of Ghetto Classics, but there were always others who sacrificed and taught and convinced the community that we were needed," Elizabeth reflected. "Simon [K.] has always done a lot of the behind-the-scenes fixing of the social issues that would otherwise make our teaching impossible. Perhaps he does not get the glory for it, but it is an essential part of what we do."

What was also proving to be essential was getting their proverbial and literal hands on instruments. What Elizabeth lacked in street cred in Korogocho she made up for in her connections and fundraising skills. During her years hustling for classical music gigs and finding money for her magazine and radio show, she had made loads of connections with powerful politicians, business people, and those within the expat community. She had no shame in going to important people and asking for favors. Growing up the daughter of a civil servant, it was second nature for her to feel comfortable using her connections to secure everything from finances to instruments. "For the kids who are in Korogocho who are the extreme polar opposite of that, it is a life and death situation," she reflected, "whereas to me, it's a phone call away to solve a problem."

While GC was allowed to borrow battered and old instruments from the Nairobi Conservatoire, they wanted to actually have a chance to own instruments that they could use whenever they needed them. As luck would have it, in March 2010, the then newly appointed German ambassador to Kenya, Margit Hellwig-Boette, heard about Ghetto Classics from Julius. While still the head of Kenyan Wildlife Service, Julius was also serving as the chairman of the Art of Music Foundation. A delegation from Bavaria, in Germany, had come to Nairobi, and Julius had helped organize a visit to Nairobi National Park for a safari. They were so grateful that later that evening at a reception at the German residence, one member of the delegation asked what they could do as a thank you. "And Julius said, 'If you want to do me a favor, help me get instruments for this newly created orchestra of slum kids,'" said Ambassador Hellwig-Boette, who later went on to serve in Bangalore, India, as the consul general for Germany. "I was the one who was the link between the two, but after half a year, it did not work out because importing instruments was not easy."

But the ambassador, who had since gotten to know Elizabeth and had seen the GC players rehearse in Korogocho, decided that she would take over the favor to get instruments for the teenagers. "If Bavarians—if my own Federal state—fails, let me see if I can do something," she said. The ambassador, every two months or so, would make private unscheduled trips to Korogocho with her husband throughout her time in Nairobi, and she felt it was important to support a project started by a local Kenyan. Over time she even got to know some of the petty criminals who hung around GC. They were equally intrigued by the diplomat who had taken a shining to the orchestra.

The ambassador reached out to the Goethe-Institut offices in Nairobi, and she was able to secure a donation of wind instruments for Ghetto Classics. It was a wonderful windfall for the program, but at times it created laughable conflict. GC members didn't get to choose which instrument to play—it was first come, first served. "They just all would try to get there first," Elizabeth said, laughing at the memory of the chaos that ensued each weekend. "I remember one girl, Josephine, she had a trumpet and one boy grabbed it away from her. Oh, the tears," she said. Elizabeth and the ambassador were also eager to get GC out and about playing concerts. The ambassador booked GC's first concert in 2011 at UN Habitat's governing council meeting in Nairobi, and also invited them to play at the German residence on German National Day on October 3, 2011. That was when the instruments were first given to GC. "Our sound was terrible, just awful," said Elizabeth. "But she did not care. She adopted us."

Another powerful ally proved to be Poland's ambassador to Kenya, Anna Grupinska. "The first time I went to Korogocho, my driver, who was Kenyan, did not want to go there," recalled Ambassador Grupinska. "He said, 'You go just for a minute, madam.' So when I was talking to Elizabeth, she told me that she had just introduced to them the wind and brass instruments. I said, 'No, it cannot be like this. Without their own instruments, [they] cannot practice.'" The Polish diplomat also good naturedly mocked that they were only playing wind and brass instruments. (Because of Kenya's colonial past, the tradition of brass bands meant things like tubas and horns were easier to get a hold of.) "'This is blowing; these are not instruments,'" Elizabeth recalled the diplomat joking during one of her visits to St. John's in 2010. Ambassador Grupinska organized a charity concert at the nearby Tribe Hotel, where they raised two thousand euros. She also helped Elizabeth apply for a Polish Aid grant, which helped GC purchase sixteen violins and cellos for the musicians.

During those days, the music lessons on weekends were pretty basic. GC members would spend an hour doing music theory (which included notation and rhythm) on the blackboard that was hung in front of the windows with a direct view over the sprawling Dandora dump. They would then be split up into smaller groups according to their instruments, and, still all in the same room, practice some of what they had just learned, including songs like "For All the Saints," "My God Is Good," and "Ainuliwe" by Kenyan songwriter Dan Em. It was loud, chaotic, and the sounds they made were more often a flurried clamor of excruciatingly off-key clanging versus anything recognizable as music.

With the influx of instruments came the pragmatic concern of where to store them. There were issues because Elizabeth and others were afraid they would be stolen and sold if they were kept overnight at St. John's, so they moved them back and forth, which proved to be complicated at times. Each week, Elizabeth, Simon K., Erick Ochieng, or a growing number of volunteers would have to transport the cellos, violins, flutes, and other instruments offsite. First, they moved them to Elizabeth's family office compound in the posh Hurlingham neighborhood, then for a time to the Mamba Village Crocodile Farm on Langata Road—owned by one of Elizabeth's friends—and later to a large container situated on a small farm allotment owned by Irene. It was guarded by a *panga*-wielding Samburu, and it is where the instruments are still kept today. It cost about five thousand Kenyan shillings (almost fifty dollars) in cab fare each week, which dug into the Art of Music's funds.

As the program continued to grow throughout 2011, Elizabeth also realized she needed to create more of a specific curriculum for the GC musicians. So she reached out to a few of her contacts, including Moses Watutua, who not only taught music at an elite Nairobi boarding school, Brookhouse, but also volunteered at the Nairobi School's music program. He agreed to not only donate books and other resources, but to also serve as the curriculum advisor for the Korogocho project. Moses initially figured he could just cut and paste curriculums he had used in the past at other schools for the GC program. "But I realized we had to make adjustments because of their social situation," Moses said of his early attempts to make the program more cohesive. "I expected things to fly as they would in a more 'normal' setting, but then I realized it was not as simple as that. And we had to be very flexible with the children's state of mind at the time, and the country's state of mind at the time."

Moses brought in some of his students from the Nairobi School—a well-known secondary school founded by the British in 1902 that had a strong music program—to help teach. Moses also soundly felt that new members entering the program should, like millions of fledgling music students across the globe, learn the basics on the recorder versus directly on the instruments like the previous cohorts had. Over time other volunteers came from the Kenyan National Youth Orchestra (KNYO), which the Art of Music Foundation helped found in 2010.

The idea for KNYO was to give young, talented musicians from across the country a chance to broaden their musical and leadership skills through three weeklong musical residencies each year. Levi was involved from the start and eventually became the musical director. But KNYO was not just about giving fourteen- to twenty-three-year-old musicians a chance to meet, practice, and perform with each other. (KNYO members have played at the United Nations in New York in 2014, and at President Barack Obama's state dinner in Nairobi in 2015.) It also over the years was to morph into being a social integration program as well. Elizabeth's long view was to give GC musicians who held promise a goal to work towards in their music. When they aged out of GC—while there is no finite end to the program, many members eventually drift off once they finish their schooling—they could move into a more professional orchestra, which they had to audition and hone their skills for.

Meanwhile, friends of GC members were becoming more and more curious as to what exactly it was that their friends were doing every Sunday. Some of the more inquisitive ones would pop in to have a nose around and decide if they wanted to be a part of what was going on. And GC members were also doing some of the recruiting. The trumpet player Samwel Otieno had not only recruited Kevin in 2012, in the previous year, he had also gotten his friend Brian Kepher to join. Born in 1994, Kepher—as he was commonly known—was one of nine children, and he spent his early years in Mathare, a slum not far from Korogocho. As a young boy, his mother was concerned about him taking up with a bad crowd of kids. She encouraged him to stick around their home and read books (his favorite being the Book of Genesis from the Old Testament) and watch movies. (He was especially fond of Bruce Lee films.) Kepher recalled being intrigued that music from some of those movies "could move my soul."

As a nine-year-old in 2003, he joined the Scouts, not because he wanted to, but out of necessity. "I was hanging out with the hooligans at school and one day we were outside when we were not supposed to be," he said. A teacher asked him what he was doing outside, so he quickly scampered away and into a nearby classroom so he wouldn't get in trouble. As it turned out, a scouting meeting was starting, and the leader, noticing that Kepher had skidded into the classroom late, asked the boy why he was there. "'I want to be a Scout,' I told the leader, but in essence, it was because I didn't want my mom to find out what I had been doing," he said, laughing.

His mother, Patricia Adhiambo, was so pleased for her son to have something to do to keep him out of trouble that she bought him a uniform. Kepher credited scouting for giving him the confidence and leadership that later on helped him become a conductor in Ghetto Classics.

In 2009, his father, a mechanic, lost his job and the family had to move to a smaller accommodation in Korogocho. Patricia sold vegetables outside the gates of St. John's to supplement the family's income, but it was not enough to cover the cost of food and housing for Kepher and his younger siblings. So his mother struck a deal with the bishop of their animism church; Kepher could stay at the church and they would feed him if he would be responsible for keeping the building tidy. The church's leader agreed and Kepher began sleeping amidst the pews at night. In 2010, he enrolled in secondary school at Our Lady of Fatima, and that same year, when preparing to march with the Scouts for a parade on Mashujaa Day (the country's National Day of Heroes in October), he happened to hear the Kenya Defense Force band rehearsing "Ee Mungu Nguvu Yetu," the Kenyan national anthem. "The first time I heard [it] it was amazing, the tension," he said. "The anthem starts with percussion and the drum. It boomed and pounded, and for me, it was a new thing born in my heart."

In March 2011, Patricia—while hawking vegetables next to ramshackle *dukas* (shops) selling used electric-plug outlets, wires, plastic piping, and secondhand shoes hung by their laces—heard incongruous sounds of music tumbling into the street. Intrigued, she was told that an orchestra made up of Korogocho teens practiced at the church. She told her son and said that the next time she heard them practicing, she would find him so he could come and check it out. By that point, Kepher had dropped out of school because he could no longer afford the fees, and when he was not cleaning up at his church he was often moping around his parents' house, helping with laundry and other household chores. After a few weeks, Patricia heard the music again, and, hoping to inspire her son out of his sulking, she called him to come to St. John's. "I ran over," he recalled.

But it took Kepher a further five months before he got up the courage, with Samwel egging him on, to join GC. When he was asked what instrument he wanted to play, Kepher immediately said percussion. He was a quick study on the snare drum and the timpani, even though in his early days in GC, Kepher would only see his percussion and music tutor every two to three months because there was not much money for GC to pay the tutor. "I was still living in the church then, and the little money that I had, instead of saving it for food, I would save it to go to the cybercafé to use the internet to go and watch videos of this great orchestra, the Berlin Philharmonic," he said. "At first, I was not watching how the conductor, the great Simon Rattle, was conducting, I was watching how the percussions were played, and that is how I learned." But over time, Kepher's attention was drawn to the conductor's podium and how Maestro Rattle and other conductors who also later became his heroes would communicate and wave with their batons, commanding respect from the orchestra and audience.

Kepher—with a round face, gapped front teeth, and vast eyes that he constantly blinked—moved with both cockiness and pride. But there were also notes of naïveté and insecurity in his carriage. While he was incredibly tenacious and smart, there was a boastfulness and boldness that could be off-putting to people. He was so eager to please people that he often changed his narrative by saying what he thought people wanted to hear as opposed to the truth. Kepher was also very guarded about his background, which at times came across almost as cagey. "He is ambitious," Elizabeth said of how Kepher's version of stories often changed, "but there is no malice in it and he is not hurting anyone."

After less than a year in GC, Kepher felt confident enough to try out for the KNYO orchestra in March 2012, and that June he also joined the Kenya Conservatoire of Music. Having proven himself to be a quick study and a self-starter, Elizabeth also committed the Art of Music Foundation to pay his school fees so that he could complete his secondary school education. Kepher, along with many of the other GC students, had also started to see that some of the things that they had to do during their Sunday music rehearsals—from being punctual for practice to working on their listening skills—had started to spill over into their schooling. Anecdotally, a number of GC students started to improve in school and become much better at their time management, both in school and in the orchestra.

But this wasn't something the fledgling musicians thought much about—they were enjoying playing music, making new friends, and gaining life-changing experiences outside Korogocho that they would have never imagined. One of those opportunities occurred when GC was invited to play on the tightly clipped lawns of the US Embassy in Nairobi. On the day of the concert, just before getting to the embassy, Kepher and his percussion-section bandmates realized they didn't have their drumsticks. But having learned early on in life that necessity was the mother of invention, scrappy Kepher and the other percussionist hatched a plan: get a few tree branches off one of the embassy trees and then use them as drumsticks. Upon arrival, however, they were given strict instructions that they were not allowed to walk across the embassy grass. Not wanting to see their plan foiled and panicking that they wouldn't be able to play, Kepher came up with an idea. They called over an escort to take one of the percussionists to the toilet. With the escort distracted, Kepher ran across the lawn, went up a tree, got a branch, and he was ready to play. "What Brian has," said Elizabeth, "is a lot of chutzpah."

But that chutzpah that he and his fellow GC musicians had developed in spades was about to be seriously tested.

Elizabeth was pregnant.

Five

Like millions of empowered women across the globe who were brought up to believe that they could have it all—a successful career and a happy family life—Elizabeth, too, had envisioned that future for herself. She had always figured at some point, after completing her education and starting her career, she would settle down, get married, and have children. But after living abroad for thirteen years and then coming back to Nairobi, scrambling to get her music programs up, running, and financed, she never quite got around to either the husband or the children. By the time she reached the cusp of her forties, she figured that, at least the having children part, was unfortunately not going to be in the cards for her.

So Elizabeth was equally extremely delighted and completely stressed to find out in August 2012 that she was unexpectedly pregnant. The news was, of course, exciting, but because of her age, her "geriatric pregnancy"—as it's commonly referred to for women over thirty-five—was considered high risk for everything from miscarriage to birth defects. While her health and the health of her baby weighed heavily on her mind, so too were her long-standing concerns that she was the backbone of everything, and with no obvious second-in-command to run things while she would be on maternity leave, things were looking dicey. And then things quickly got even more precarious. "To the doctor, it was the miracle of miracles," she said. "But then I started spotting at six weeks and both he and my mother said to me, 'Is work more important than your child? You decide; the choice is yours.'"

Elizabeth obviously agreed that her unborn child took priority over all else and so she acquiesced, mostly, to her doctor's orders that she go on bed rest, which meant that while she was not officially confined to her bed, she had to take things easy. For the first few months she mostly hung around the house, but, "of course, I would sneak out and check on them." She had asked her friend Duncan Wambugu, whom she used to perform recitals with around Nairobi, to be in charge of the administrative aspects of GC. But her friend—who had recently come back from the US after completing a PhD in music education—was a lecturer in music at Kenyatta University, so he was often feeling pulled in conflicting directions. GC classes and events often happened serendipitously without much notice or planning, which proved difficult sometimes given Duncan's teaching schedule at university. Meanwhile, Father John had promised Elizabeth that as long as the foundation paid for the fuel, GC could have access to his car to pick up the instruments each weekend. But as Elizabeth and the GC members soon found, that sometimes proved difficult when there wasn't money for petrol.

GC was also still in serious financial trouble. Since its creation at the end of 2009, the Art of Music Foundation relied on donations from individuals who believed in what they were trying to do in Korogocho and also with KNYO. The foundation's board, made up of five people, including Julius, Rachel, and Irene, each month would personally contribute one hundred dollars to the foundation. But money was always tight, and with Elizabeth unable to go out and fundraise much during her pregnancy, GC was soon just running on financial fumes. It was a tough time for Elizabeth personally as well. "I was not working and I had no income," she recalled, adding that she had to ask her parents for help. "I was not married, I was pregnant, I left this stable pharmacy job to do this 'nonsense' thing and now I had no money."

It was also incredibly daunting for Simon K. too, who, because Duncan and Father John were not able to help out as much as planned, felt he had to take up the mantle to run GC's activities. He'd seen the difference that the music program had made not only to his life (he was now an obsessed saxophonist), but also for the dozens of kids who each week would come to practice, have some food, and find a safe space away from their burdens. Over the years, many people within Korogocho had also come to appreciate what GC was doing.

"We built a cohesive community," said Simon K. "And maybe they were not so interested in what we were doing in terms of music, but that we were doing something for the kids."

Though other members and volunteer teachers were helping, the vast majority of the pressure fell on Simon K.'s busy shoulders. "It was Simon, one hundred percent," Elizabeth said, referring to who was really running the show in her absence. When she went on leave, things really started to crumble and Simon K. became seriously depressed. Not only was he having to constantly cajole Father John and others in the parish to get rehearsal rooms at St. John's (the office and practice space that GC eventually moved into was not completed until 2015), but Simon K. was also working two jobs. He did odd gigs in construction and part-time social work with street children for European Committee for Agricultural Training (CEFA), an Italian NGO. He was making eighty dollars a month, and some of that money was going to fund GC. "If the program collapsed on my side, the youths would laugh at me," Simon K. said. "But I had to keep everything secret because I knew Elizabeth was frustrated." It was a constant battle that Simon K. was dealing with, and he found that he even didn't have time for his beloved saxophone because of all the stress.

While Simon K. was trying to run the overall organization, GC members like Kepher and Samwel, who were also members of KNYO, rolled up their proverbial sleeves and were helping both to teach others while also working on improving their own musicianship. "We as the senior members started picking up some of the leadership roles and filling in with teaching and lessons," Kepher recalled. "The leadership started growing from within. And people started feeling like, 'Yeah, we are a part of this,' and they started giving and sharing their ideas of how things should go." Samwel also found he really enjoyed teaching the younger kids how to play and read music. "I love music and I loved when I shared my ideas with those kids, you know?" said Samwel.

Born in 1994, Samwel was raised in Korogocho, the only child of his parents' union, and had attended primary school at St. John's. "As you can see around Korogocho, there are a lot of groups of bad people but I wanted to avoid those groups, so that is why I joined the choir," Samwel recalled with a slight smile that revealed a gold-plated front tooth. "It is a really dangerous neighborhood and I just used to tell myself, 'I should not be here; I should be somewhere else.'" When GC received an initial donation of battered brass instruments, Samwel was immediately smitten. "They called me," he said, referring to the instruments. "I liked the color, the shape, the sound, but my favorite was the trumpet."

Elizabeth was drawn to Samwel because she could see that he had a raw talent for not only his trumpet playing but for teaching as well. "He was one of the first members, and he held great potential even then, and if he would have stuck it out, he would have been very good," she said. Samwel showed so much potential that Elizabeth arranged for him to get private lessons from Moses. Samwel also had a broken front tooth, and Elizabeth was told that he would not be able to play as well if it was not fixed, so she paid for him to get it taken care of at the dentist. But after one school holiday, Samwel didn't come back to GC. She had heard from his friends that he had moved away, up to Kisumu (about 340 kilometers northwest from Nairobi), to stay with his father and stepmother. Elizabeth was gutted he had left the program and when she received a phone call from him several months later, she was compelled to help him.

Samwel told her that his stepmother had kicked him out. Since then, he had been forced to live on the streets of Kisumu and he was desperate to come back to Nairobi, but even more especially to Ghetto Classics. The bleeding heart in Elizabeth kicked in, and after talking it over with her friend Judy, who was also on the foundation's board, it was decided that Elizabeth would send Samwel five hundred Kenyan shillings (about five dollars) each week for food, and she started paying for his secondary school fees out of her own pocket. Her only requirement was that he come to GC each week to teach and play. For Samwel, who loved music, it was not a big ask. "I was a changed person because of GC," Samwel reminisced. Glad to be off the streets, back in school, and again a part of his beloved GC, things started looking up for Samwel.

But about a year later when Elizabeth was seven months pregnant,

Samwel found himself in trouble again—this time of his own making. The headmaster of his school, who somehow found out that Elizabeth was the one covering the trumpet player's school fees (each term she would give the money directly to Samwel to pay), called her to ask why she had not yet paid. Elizabeth was incredulous, explaining to the headmaster that she had given the money, per usual, to Samwel and it was the first she had heard of his delinquent fees. The headmaster verified that no money had come in, and, fuming, Elizabeth went with Simon K. to the school to find out what was going on.

Upon arrival at the school located near Kariobangi, Elizabeth also learned from the headmaster that Samwel had started a riot there, making a claim that the headmaster had not registered his students with the National Examinations Council for their Kenya-wide tests. The headmaster told her that he was kicking Samwel out of school. She began berating Samwel. "Are you crazy?" she asked him, shaking with rage and bitterly disappointed that he had lied to her and caused so much trouble. Recalling the incident several years later, Elizabeth laughed, thinking what it must have looked like to a passerby: a heavily pregnant middle-class middle-aged woman loudly arguing with a slum kid. "I was thinking, 'My goodness, I have problems of my own,'" she recalled. "I have a child in my belly and I am here yelling at him, sitting on this uncomfortable bench." Samwel explained to her that he had been sharing a bed with three other boys in a room, but they had moved out, so he used the school fees to buy himself a bed. After that incident, Samwel dropped out of GC for two months, hanging around, not doing much of anything except scavenging from time to time in the dump site. "I understood why she yelled at me," Samwel said. "She did not trust me."

It was to be a forewarning of things to come.

In May 2013, a month after Uhuru Kenyatta—the son of Kenya's first president, Jomo Kenyatta—was elected president for the first time, Elizabeth gave birth to a healthy, lively baby girl that she named Wanjiku. As most new mothers find after their first child is born, in the beginning it was a roller coaster of emotions and a messy assembly line of diapers and feedings. "Those first few months, you don't know which way is up," said Elizabeth, reflecting on that spring and summer of 2013. "And as for GC, there was no money and no direction."

Simon K. was also feeling rudderless. For one reason or another, a number of GC members had dropped out—including Samwel—and recruitment had come to almost a standstill. Hoping to bring in new members, Simon K. tried to get kids who were scavenging in the dump site to come and have a few music lessons at St. John's. "I would say to them, 'I will buy you lunch, come and learn,'" he said. "I did not want to see the program fail; I had seen other projects fail, and I was not assured the program would go on, as no one was directly supporting it."

Luckily for Simon K., when Moses came back from an extended vacation in the UK—where he had visited contacts at the Concordia Foundation, a music and arts charity—he realized on a visit to St. John's that things had almost completely unraveled and that Simon K. was in a desperate state. "I had to get him off the building sites," Moses said. "I had to get him out of there and encourage him, and I told him, 'We cannot allow this to fail because Liz is not here.'" Moses was able to secure some funding from Concordia to not only help pay for lessons, but also to get more teachers in.

He also gave Simon K. a small stipend of two thousand dollars, which Simon K. said felt like a small fortune. "I had never touched such kind of money in my life," Simon K. said, adding that he was given the cash in a small brown envelope. Moses also reorganized the curriculum to get things going again.

One of the teachers who had been with GC since 2011 and had stuck it out during those dark days was Benjamin Wamocho, who later became GC's musical director. Known by everyone simply as Wamocho, he had come to Nairobi in 2006 to attend the Nairobi School. He had grown up in rural Bungoma County, in western Kenya, and he always said that if he had not found music, he would have been perfectly happy herding goats and cows along the vast dry Kenyan savannah. After completing secondary school, Wamocho began studies to be a vet at the University of Nairobi, but music was his true love. "I do not think I will be a veterinarian; I am too dependent on music, and my heart is here," Wamocho said, touching his moustache as he looked around the amphitheater at St. John's and watched as the orchestra loudly practiced the song "Oye" by Jim Papoulis.

When KNYO was founded in 2010, Moses recruited his former student to be a librarian for the music, making him something of a Mr. Fix-It who dealt with everything from reprimanding kids who were running late to replacing missing music sheets that kids had forgotten at home. Wamocho then became one of the original KNYO tutors to come to GC. "But I had these other skills and so my job here just grew and grew," he said. From the start, Wamocho believed in what Ghetto Classics was trying to do, not just as a music program but also for the wider Korogocho community. It was why he had stuck it out even when things started to fall apart. "This is not just a job, but a responsibility," he said. "I believe what we do here is bigger than me, bigger than Elizabeth. It is an idea whose time has come, and I think GC will be around a long time after I have gone."

When Elizabeth came back from maternity leave in August 2013, she was prepared for an uphill battle, though she also knew that she had dedicated support from people like Simon K. and Wamocho, who despite and because of all the trials, had both become more galvanized and invested in what GC was doing. "I was like, 'What the fuck are we going to do? How are we going to pick this up? Is this really what I should be doing?'" she recalled. "It was difficult, I had no funding. It was all personal financing, so essentially from Wanjiku's diaper money." Julius, who was on the board and had fallen in love with classical music as a teen while in boarding school, where Beethoven and Bach were played during school assembly every evening, put it more succinctly: "We wobbled but we somehow held it together."

One of the priorities, aside from trying to secure a steadier funding stream, was getting fresh blood into GC. There was now a huge gap in ages between those who had been in the initial few cohorts back in 2008 and 2009 and those who they were recruiting new to the program in 2013. One of the very few new members who had joined GC that year—who would go on to become a vital member of the GC orchestra and staff—was a fifteen-year-old tall, graceful girl named Celine Akumu. Born and raised in Korogocho, Celine had three brothers and one sister. "It was not a pleasant childhood," Celine said, sporting a whitewashed denim jacket and a small Diamante stud in her nose. "There are a lot of challenges, lots of gangsters, but that is what I know. It is, after all, my community."

Her father was deeply worried about raising his daughters in such a dangerous place. "It was one of my dad's biggest concerns," she said. "He did not want me to get involved with bad stuff." Her father died in 2010, and her mother made ends meet by running a *duka* selling things like soda and sweets. When she was a ten-year-old in primary school, Celine was sent away to boarding school in Kisumu and then moved on to another boarding school, also outside of Nairobi, until she was in form three. During one of her school holidays when she was back home, a friend of hers who was a trombonist in GC told her about the music program.

She had always wanted to be an actress and had been encouraged to apply for a scholarship to study acting in Poland. But her mother forbade her to go. Back to finish up her secondary schooling at Riverside Academy in Nairobi—where she was a below average student who struggled with basic reading and writing—and upset she could not pursue acting, Celine thought about trying her hand at music. "I was amazed to find my contemporaries were playing instruments and it was so cool," she said. At first she was drawn to the violin, but when she joined GC there were not enough violins to go around, so one of the tutors recommended that she try the clarinet instead. She was a bit disappointed at first, but, "I fell in love with the clarinet slowly."

With an injection of new members and some older GC members starting to come back, Elizabeth was determined to carry on. And then she got a phone call that completely changed the trajectory of Ghetto Classics. Safaricom, the telecom company that had supported Elizabeth's magazine all those years ago, was planning to start a jazz festival the following February. The festival director reached out to Elizabeth, saying they were thinking of doing something and that GC was one of the nonprofits that the company would support through the money raised from ticket sales. "She told me that she was not promising anything, but she asked for a write-up of what GC did, and she would get back to me," Elizabeth said.

A few weeks later, another Safaricom executive, Zaheeda Suleman, who was the head of the company's events and sponsorships, also reached out to Elizabeth, telling her that they wanted to start the Safaricom Youth Orchestra (SYO) and wondered whether she would be interested in running it. Elizabeth rightly thought that it could be a great opportunity for the GC members to interact with kids from all different backgrounds. Joining SYO could be a goal to work towards and a way to continue to improve their musicianship.

So she said yes.

Six

If Arun Ghosh didn't have a clarinet in his left hand and a long, flowing burgundy kurta tunic over his black trousers, he could have passed for a DJ spinning tunes at a wild clubbing gig in Ibiza or Miami.

As the Indian-born, British-raised musician and composer jumped up and down, flailing his right hand in the air, yelling at the crowd to "get up," he started madly playing "Dagger Dance" on his shiny black clarinet. The crowd got even more riled up into a musical frenzy. Then, as the Nairobi Horns began blasting notes from their brass instruments that thudded and boomed through the loudspeakers, Hussein Misambi, a captivating Tanzanian drummer playing along with the other musicians on stage, grinned ear to ear as he started his rap. The audience went mad for the hip-hop and pop-infused beats, screaming and jumping up and down, following Arun's orchestrated lead.

It was a Tusker beer-tinged Sunday afternoon in February 2017, the sun shining down hot at the Moi International Sports Centre. As Arun danced and sweated up on the stage in the main tent, expat women in long maxi dresses and trendy sunglasses chased after their children in T-shirts and Crocs across prickly, dry, brown grass. Hipster Kenyan men in fedoras and flip-flops conversed with European and Asian diplomats as they stood in line at stalls selling wine, beer, *nyama choma* (barbecued meat), and fries. Over at the Embassy of Israel tent, there were succulent kebabs and thick tahini to nibble on while guests milled around picking up free samples of Dead Sea moisturizers. The Belgians, not to be outdone, were peddling chocolates and white beer and offering free tumblers for anyone who correctly answered quiz questions about their country. (Sample question: "What is the name of the current monarch?" The answer was Philippe of Belgium. In 2019 several of the GC saxophonists including Simon K. and Erick Ochieng performed for his wife, Queen Mathilde, on her trip to Kenya.) Meanwhile, ticketholders who had VIP passes could take shade—and free sparkling wine—in tents sponsored by various local and international sponsors including the Kempinski and Intercontinental hotels groups.

The fourth annual Safaricom Jazz Festival lineup for the rest of the afternoon included Congolese music legend Ray Lema, Israel's female singing trio The Hazelnuts, and the American saxophonist and six-time Grammy winner David Sanborn. Meanwhile, the Ghetto Classics orchestra, which was the direct beneficiary of money made from the event (according to Safaricom, that year's ticket sales yielded $150,000), had performed earlier in the day in a rather unfortunate opening slot of 12:00 p.m., with Kepher handling conducting duties.

After they performed, Emily and Martha checked out all the free food and product samples on offer. They talked a little bit about how strange it was that all these people were here, in part, to support Safaricom's efforts for Ghetto Classics. They laughed at how many of the people sipping champagne and eating canapés in their linen shirts and billowy dresses would be aghast if they saw where the GC musicians lived, which as the crow flies, was quite close. The performing musicians, however, had a much deeper understanding. That was because one of the requirements for all those who had accepted invitations to play at the festival was that they give tutorials to the GC musicians, either at St. John's or one of the rehearsal spaces set up during the lead-up to the festival. (David Sanborn met some of the GC kids at his hotel.)

For Arun, who had chosen to go to Korogocho to meet the budding musicians, just getting to St. John's had been an eye-opening experience. Though he had spent a lot of time in places like Mumbai and Calcutta, he had never actually been to the guts of a slum before. "You go on this bumpy, winding road past little shops and businesses, seeing people just living and working there," he said, sitting in the British Council tent on the afternoon of the festival, his battered clarinet box at his feet, and sporting a black short-sleeve T-shirt that showed off several tattoos on his arms. "And it just heightened my awareness once I got to St. John's of just what a wonderful thing was happening there in terms of bringing music into that place. There was an absolute joy that has come into the area through the beauty of music. It was like flowers growing."

Celine, Erick, and a few of the other GC tutors and members were doing an impromptu jam while they waited for Arun to show up in Korogocho, and once he arrived, they played a few folk tunes together. Arun was handed a recorder—the instrument he had first learned on—and he played some music with some of the younger kids who were just starting to read notes. As he ran his hands through his onyx black hair, which was shaved on both sides but long in the front, Arun recalled that it was a lovely introduction to Ghetto Classics. During that visit, he asked some of the more advanced students to play something for him. "And they started playing one of their compositions, and this is something really important for me because I feel that if musicians want to progress, they have to begin writing their own music," he said, adding that he personally started to transition as a musician once he stopped playing jazz standards and started composing his own work. "I feel like there are a lot of improvisers and composers in the making there."

That was music to Safaricom CEO Bob Collymore's ears.

A lifelong fan of jazz, Bob had been born and raised in Guyana before moving to London as a teen. He had risen up the ranks of Vodafone, and in 2010 he took over the helm of Safaricom from Michael Joseph. "I never had the opportunity to learn music," he said over lunch in London's Covent Garden a month after the festival, while he was in town on a business trip. "My parents could not afford it but I always wanted to. But I created the opportunity for my son to learn music and now he is a keen musician." It was on a trip to Sweden in early 2013, where Bob had been invited by the Swedish royal family to take part in the World Youth and Child Forum, that he first got inspired to start the SYO after seeing a concert for conference attendees put on by children from an international music college. "And I thought, 'Why don't we have this in Kenya?'" he said, leaning his tall back away from the table. "I thought we should do something about that. Because surely we should be able to provide instruments and show children what good music sounds like."

Bob's musician son had been to St. John's a few times to check out GC and reported back to his father that what was happening there was fantastic. It was something that had stuck in the CEO's mind so that when the notion came to him to found an orchestra, his thought was to not just get the best teenage musicians in and around Nairobi (unlike KNYO, which meets only a few times a year, SYO practices every Saturday), but to also help give some of the GC kids a boost in terms of improving their musicianship. "We decided that we would bring together these children who are living in the most desperate conditions with similarly talented kids from more privileged backgrounds," Bob reflected. "After all, music doesn't really recognize economic boundaries, so why should we?"

A few months after his return from Sweden, Bob met Jef Neve, a Belgian jazz pianist who had come to Nairobi to perform a solo show at the Michael Joseph Centre at Safaricom's headquarters. After his performance, Jef, his manager Pieter Kindt, and Bob spoke about the jazz scene in Nairobi, and from that conversation the idea for a jazz festival was born. (Jef not only came back to perform at the third Safaricom Jazz Festival in 2016 alongside other musicians, including Branford Marsalis and South African musician and activist Hugh Masekela, but he and Pieter also helped to raise money to donate one hundred instruments to GC that were sent via shipping container from Belgium to Kenya in 2018.) After that initial conversation, Bob's team got to work on organizing the event and soon discovered that since they had generous sponsors for the festival, they would have a net profit from the ticket sales. "It was then that we completed the circle through linking this festival with the work of Art of Music," Bob stated. In addition to providing those much-needed funds for the project, it was also important that the musicians from Ghetto Classics met with the international performers. Bob said it put some "real meaning" in the festival.

To Bob and his colleagues, it seemed a natural progression that part of the company's social outreach would have a music focus given Safaricom's history of supporting events like Classical Fusions, which Elizabeth had helped organize over the years. However, Bob strongly disliked calling GC a corporate social responsibility project.

"For us it is not CSR," he said, taking a sip of white wine to wash down his fish cakes. "The first word in CSR is 'corporate,' which does not resonate that well for us."

Safaricom's unconventional view of their outreach also meant that they were more relaxed from the start with how the money for GC was spent and weren't insistent on getting statistics—which Elizabeth didn't have—on the program's growth. "You can imagine how difficult that can be," said Elizabeth when asked how she accounted for the money they received from Safaricom and other supporters. "For some kids we buy food every month, we go out on the street, we get a bunch of this and that, but in kiosks they don't have receipts. Or I give our social worker, Peter Kuria, money to give to one of the kids because the young man doesn't have shoes. I have to trust that it gets done because there will be no receipt."

Elizabeth was grateful for Safaricom's support, but at first she wasn't quite sure what it all meant since there had never been a jazz festival before and she didn't know what kind of money they were talking about. "I did not know what kind of commitment they were giving me, so to me it was just an injection of cash," she said. "In those days, 100,000 Kenyan shillings [$1,000] would keep us going for three months, so I was ecstatic when the first five million Kenyan shillings [$50,000] came in February 2014." (Originally Safaricom signed on to support GC for three years, and then in 2017, after the partnership proved successful, they extended the contract for another three.) That money not only meant that GC could get more instruments and expand the program by doing more recruitment—Simon M., Kamau, and Teddy all joined that year—but also they could pay teachers and add some staff. Simon K., who had worked so hard over the years as both a member of GC and then as the ad hoc director when Elizabeth was on maternity leave, was officially given a full-time job to run the day-to-day operations at St. John's.

After that inaugural jazz festival in 2014—the headliner that year was Cameroonian jazz bassist Richard Bona with supporting acts, including Israeli saxophonist Yuval Cohen, the Rhythm Junks from Belgium, and Kenyan jazz guitarist Eddie Grey—Bob, Elizabeth, and the Safaricom staff turned their focus to forming SYO. In March they held auditions—Celine, Samwel, Kevin, and Kepher all got places—and Duncan Wambugu was named musical director because of his strong background in conducting and music education. In April, SYO officially launched. "It was all a bit, 'Whooo-hooo,'" said Elizabeth, laughing and shaking her head at the memory.

SYO was a great opportunity for a number of the GC members, not only because at Safaricom headquarters where they held their practices, they had access to to a safe, clean space to practice their music each Saturday, but they were also guaranteed hot lunches like lentil curry and chapattis (for some, that was their only food all day) and a chance to meet other teens who they would likely never have spoken to if not for the opportunity to play music with each other. Some of these teens were the children of wealthy Kenyans, while others were expat kids whose parents held high positions in United Nations organizations, embassies, and multinational companies. However, just like pretty much any school cafeteria across the globe, there were cliques, and the kids often didn't mix much during lunch or while they had breaks from their sectionals with professional teachers that were held in various conference rooms scattered across the large building. So most of the GC kids tended to just hang around with each other. In the early days, Bob got some pushback from middle-class parents who weren't keen for their children to be hanging around with the slum kids. "I remember there were some kids who did not want to eat with other kids, and I said, 'You come and you eat your food, no one is better,'" he reminisced, adding also that some of the other kids didn't want to work with the GC kids because they smelled. "And I said, 'Yeah, they do smell. So do you want to stay in the orchestra?'"

But over time, some friendships did develop. Simon M., for example, after winning a slot in SYO six months after joining GC, got to know another trombonist named Stella, who came from a middle-class background. When he started, she was first trombone, but over time, in part because she was busy applying to universities and did not have as much time to practice her music, Simon M. became first trombone for SYO. "Her background is totally different from my own, but through music, we are one," he recalled. "She has expanded my musical ideas."

In the spring of 2014, KNYO was invited to send a handful of their musicians on a cultural exchange program to run in tandem during the Commonwealth Games—an international multisport event with participant athletes coming from the Commonwealth of Nations—being held in Glasgow that summer. Eager to expand the musical horizons for her musicians, Elizabeth was told that the Scokendia Ensemble would be made up of twenty-six young musicians from Scotland, Kenya, and India. The ensemble would tour across Scotland during the Games, showcasing music from all three countries as well as premiering pieces from three commissioned composers from each of the countries.

Along with David Ralak, a talented violinist who would eventually become the Nairobi Orchestra's concertmaster, as well as a few other young KNYO musicians, Elizabeth and Levi picked Celine and Kepher to participate. But getting passports and visas was not an easy task because neither of them had birth certificates. When Celine's mother was asked by Elizabeth about whether she had any documentation for her daughter's birth, she replied, "Why do you need that? You can see that she is alive." It was a ton of work for Elizabeth to coordinate. But those skills she picked up from dealing with embassies and government offices to get the documents would come in handy when she would have to pull off similar feats in later years when other GC members were invited to travel internationally to summer music camps and festivals.

On the day the musicians were supposed to fly out in July—with all the documents sorted out and passports, visas, and airline tickets in hand—a massive glitch that had not been caught beforehand almost ended Celine's dreams to travel to Scotland. The chaperone called Levi from the airport in Nairobi to say that they weren't going to let her on the flight because there was an issue with her passport. Levi told the rest of them to get on the flight and he came to pick her up. The problem was over Celine's name. Not knowing how strict the airlines were when it came to documentation, Celine had given her nickname, Pinkie, when her ticket was booked, which obviously did not match her passport. So the airline refused to let her check in. The next day, a Saturday, Celine went to SYO practice to wait to see if things could be sorted out. "Celine had her bags with her and all the GC kids were making fun of her, saying, 'So this is Scotland,' and she was so depressed and embarrassed," said Levi. "But Elizabeth did her magic, and so Celine was booked out on another flight."

With that problem solved, Celine was ready to head out. But both Elizabeth and Levi were concerned that, having never travelled before and with a layover in Amsterdam, she needed a crash course in airport protocols and procedures. What may seem like second nature to frequent fliers could be a minefield for first-time air travelers, especially someone like Celine. She was not only a minor, but a kid from the slums who might be easily overwhelmed when it came to everything from asking directions to going from one gate to another and getting through passport control.

So Levi sat down with Celine at the airport and explained the process, in great detail. "Levi prepared me so well," Celine said, adding that a few years later she had gone to Australia for a musical exchange program and that process had been smooth. Just as Elizabeth over the years grew accustomed to finagling birth certificates and other documents for her GC kids, Levi, too, would often repeat his airport talk with members of GC who were travelling abroad on their own or in a small group.

Once in Scotland, Celine and Kepher had an incredible time playing across the country and interacting with people from all walks of life and cultures. "I was so excited and happy, and things were so different, things I had only ever seen on television," Celine said. They explored different kinds of food on the trip—she enjoyed trying a kangaroo burger but was not impressed with Chinese food—and bonded with other members of the ensemble.

"For Celine as well, I think it boosted her confidence a lot to be with musicians from around the world, though I think maybe she missed home a bit more," said Jamie Munn, a Scottish musician who came up with the Scokendia concept after spending years working on music projects in Kenya, India, Hong Kong, and Germany.

For Kepher, the thrill was more in the audiences and musical aspects he picked up along the way. What he particularly remembered from his time in Scotland was that was where he was first inspired to compose his own music and work on arrangements. "Because when you compose you are not playing someone else's music, and so I figured I could try," he said, echoing Arun Ghosh's thoughts.

That trip to Scotland also proved seminal for Kepher because it gave him the travel bug that would later take him to Gabon, Germany, Switzerland, Tanzania, South Korea, and the United States. "I think the biggest reaction from Kepher was him realizing what a big world is out there," Jamie said. "Kepher seemed bamboozled by the 'liberal' nature of people and I think it was eye-opening for him in many respects." While in Glasgow the musicians were taken to see *Madame Butterfly* and a one-off concert where the BBC Scottish Symphony and Royal Scottish National orchestras joined together to make a huge orchestra with Nicola Benedetti as soloist. The overall trip seemed to light a fire in Kepher. In fact, he was so enthused that—in typical bravehearted Kepher fashion—he marched into the principal's office at the Royal Conservatoire of Scotland where the outgoing principal and the incoming one were having a meeting and asked them if he could get a scholarship to study.

One of the reasons that Celine had been chosen to go to Scotland was because she had shown strong leadership within the program. Earlier in the year she had proactively asked Elizabeth if she would periodically meet with female members of GC. The idea was for Elizabeth to not only to talk with them about their music; those conversations would also be a safe space where they could discuss the personal issues they were facing in their lives in everything from schooling to hygiene issues. It was during one of those sessions that Elizabeth remembered meeting a young percussionist named Precious Adiambo[2] for the first time. The troubled young teen told Elizabeth that when her godmother's husband was drunk, he would chase her around the house. "I will never forget that conversation," Elizabeth said, her face quite taut and serious.

Precious, it seemed, was all alone in the world. Born in 1998, not only did she not know what day she was born but she also did not know her father. Born in Korogocho, Precious's mother made

---

2 Her name has been changed to protect her identity.

chang'aa and was also an alcoholic. Like a number of women who brewed, she also quite likely sold sex for money, which was probably how she contracted AIDS. She died when Precious was twelve (three of her other brothers had also died, but Precious never explained the causes), while another brother who was mentally disabled was taken care of in western Kenya. She then went to live with her godmother with the horrible husband. "I had never met anyone who had no one and nothing in the world," Elizabeth said. "And that is the day that she became mine." Elizabeth started to take a more concerted interest in Precious, not only in terms of her music but her home life as well.

* * *

In September 2014, Eric Booth, who at the time was in the midst of visiting a number of global Sistema-inspired programs for research for his book, *Playing for Their Lives: The Global El Sistema Movement for Social Change Through Music,* came to Korogocho.[3] He was enthused by what he saw and was struck not only by how dire the situation was for the GC members, but also the enthusiasm they showed when playing their instruments. "In other countries, kids are joyful and having good experiences but it is not quite as radiant," he said. "If you want to have a feeling of how fun it can be to make music with your friends, just go see it work, because there is an exuberance that shines so bright in contrast to the physical surroundings. That when you have to brush the dirt from the smog off your violin every ten minutes, and then you are having a hilariously fun time getting set up for the run through of your next piece of music, it is so stark and unusually dramatic."

Eric was also taken with how the SYO was a mixture of kids from

---

3 El Sistema is a publicly financed music education program founded in Caracas, Venezuela, in 1975 by late economist and conductor José Antonio Abreu. Though not originally targeted towards at-risk youth, it has become an example for music education programs in disadvantaged communities across the globe. However, by the 1990s, the program, which includes the renowned Simón Bolívar Symphony Orchestra (SBSO), began promoting itself as a social project aimed at helping poor youth through musical instruction.

such diverse and disparate backgrounds playing together in an orchestra. "It does not happen much in [Sistema-inspired] programs where you get opportunities to put separate worlds together in a way that is very promising for long-term relationship development," he said. During his brief time in Nairobi, Eric not only quickly bonded with Elizabeth, but he also got to know Celine, Wamocho, and Kepher. He was especially struck by how much Kepher, who was newly inspired since his Scotland trip, believed that his mission in life was to be the next Gustavo Dudamel, the acclaimed Venezuelan-born conductor and violinist who had been a member of El Sistema as a teen.

Eric had a long conversation with Kepher after a special KNYO rehearsal, which was held to help five of their members who were preparing to go to New York. Those musicians would be performing with a five-country gathering of musicians from Sistema-inspired programs at the United Nations, sponsored by Chinese pianist Lang Lang's foundation. Though only a few were going, the KNYO members wanted to rehearse with them to help the five get the full orchestral feel for the music they were practicing. Eric and Kepher got to talking on a variety of subjects, with Kepher asking Eric about everything from the El Sistema program in Venezuela to how much did conductors study their scores and could he get into a workshop with Gustavo. He also asked Eric about book publishing. "He had these ideas that he thinks belong in a book so he grilled me in his naïve but earnest way to know everything he could that might set him up to write a book about how he sees the musical world," Eric recalled. "And as uninformed as his ideas would be given his background, the quality of his inquiry was powerful."

Meanwhile, there was a big change at St. John's when Father John, who had originally spearheaded the idea of a youth music program, moved on to do missionary work in another part of Kenya. When appointed to the position six years previously, the priest had come to Korogocho with new ideas and had integrated himself into the slum, committed to helping the people that he served. Father John had also been very good at getting fundraising from international donors and had even received a Franco-German human rights award in recognition for his work in Korogocho.

Though Father John's work with GC had waned since its founding, he still supported what the program was trying to do within the community, and pretty much let GC have free reign to use the classrooms and the amphitheater for practices, concerts, and tours for potential donors. Later based in the northern Kenyan region of Turkana, Father John stated in a 2018 email that even all these years later he still kept "abreast of [their] activities, and I remain proud [of] having helped found GC." After Father John left, his replacement was not as generous with the parish facilities—including the now-finished community center building—which was not only used by musicians for music theory and recorder lessons, but was also office space for GC.

"He kept fighting me," Simon K. said angrily about the new priest. "He gave me an invoice for thirty thousand Kenyan shillings [$300], so I had to push back. I told him, 'It is used for the kids; I don't know why you are asking for this money.'"

Simon K. told the father that GC had not only become a strong part of St. John's fabric, it was also part of Korogocho's as a whole. He pleaded with the priest, arguing that for children, GC served as a shelter away from all that was lying in wait just beyond the parish gates. Wasn't protecting children and lifting them out of a life of poverty all part and parcel of what the priest and the Comboni Missionaries aimed to do in the slum? The priest finally relented, but relations never improved between the two men.

* * *

In January 2015, Salut Salon, an all-female chamber music quartet made up of two violinists, a cellist, and a pianist from Hamburg, Germany, came on tour to Nairobi on invitation from a friend who was the deputy headmaster of the German School Nairobi. The quartet had a reputation for fun and had been dubbed by one music journalist as the "Harlem Globetrotters [of] string quartets" because of their unconventional and lighthearted performances of classical pieces. Some of their musical hijinks included the two violinists chasing each other around on stage while performing pieces from composers like Vivaldi. The musicians were keen to support a local

Kenyan charity and when they came across the Art of Music Foundation on the internet, they reached out, asking Ghetto Classics to perform with them; their concert at the Michael Joseph Centre raised seven hundred thousand Kenyan shillings [$7,000] for GC.

The women from Salut Salon also headed out to Korogocho, and while there they noticed that the GC string musicians lacked a lot of basics when it came to music theory and technique. During their visit to GC, the young musicians inundated the women with questions on everything from the best way to properly tune a violin to how to play staccato. Once back home in Germany, violinist Angelika Bachmann, one of the founding members of Salut Salon, kept trying to figure out ways that they could bring teachers over from Europe to Korogocho. And then she and Stephanie Schiller, a violinist who handled media enquiries for the quartet, hit upon an idea: they could organize weekly lessons over Skype for the string students. Salut Salon used the money that they had raised from their Nairobi concert to pay for the teachers, whom they hired in both Germany and Armenia.

The first Skype class they held in June 2015 had six students, and since all of them were also SYO members, the weekly lessons were held at Safaricom. When that money ran out, Stephanie and Salut Salon continued to fundraise, and Stephanie started doing the lessons on her own every Saturday morning. Over the years, the group grew to about twenty-five musicians. Kevin was eventually charged with organizing the calls and getting the kids' times slotted in and ready for their lessons. Those video calls not only became an integral part of learning for the Kenyan string musicians, but also an important thing for Stephanie as well. "When I stay with my boyfriend on a Friday night, I go home at 8:00 a.m. the next morning so I can Skype," she said. "It is part of my life." During the first two years, she focused almost solely on intonation. "I would say, 'Again, again, again,' and I had to scream my words to tell them where to put their fingers to sound the right way," she reminisced. "They had to learn how to tune their instruments, everything from their Skype screens, and it was hard work." This, of course, was all pre-Covid, so at the time it seemed quite unconventional to hold music sessions online.

* * *

With Simon K. handling things on the ground at St. John's, another much-needed infusion of cash coming from the second Jazz Festival, and SYO running smoothly with Duncan at the helm, Elizabeth figured that it was a good time to do some networking outside of Kenya. Having kept in touch with Eric Booth, the New York-based educator, since his visit the year before, Elizabeth reached out to him in order to grow the Art of Music Foundation. It was not only important for her to see how youth music programs and orchestras were being run in the US, it would also give her a chance to get some perspective and ideas of where she wanted to take the foundation.

In June, after attending a youth orchestra conference in Cleveland, she met Eric in New York, where he introduced Elizabeth to Joanna Massey, the director of Carnegie Hall's learning and engagements division. Joanna's staff ran Link Up, a global program that teaches music to young people by having them play with local orchestras. Upon hearing about the program, Elizabeth was inspired, thinking it might be a way to grow the GC program not only within other schools in Korogocho, but also into other disadvantaged areas across Nairobi. "We offer it free all over the world, and it is for whoever feels it is the right fit for what they are doing," said Joanna. "We really were not looking for outreach but Elizabeth said, 'I think this program will have value.'" So the Art of Music Foundation became the first—and as of 2022, still the only—African partner with Link Up.

It was a huge coup for Elizabeth and the Art of Music Foundation, not only in terms of bettering the already existing program with a new curriculum, but it also meant that it now had strong links with one of the world's most preeminent music organizations and was part of a network that expanded from Colombia to China. Bob was excited by the prospect too because he had started to think that GC should be scaling up so that Safaricom's outreach could be seen in other parts of Kenya as well. "If the principle is that music moves, then why not expand it?" he said, adding that as a concept, GC programs could be implemented with local business partners outside of Kenya as well. "How can we help Elizabeth to package this in a box and then take it to [Nigeria], to Tanzania, and other places?"

Towards the end of 2015, while Elizabeth was busy starting the program in six schools across Nairobi, the GC musicians from Orchestra A who were in the performing orchestra began rehearsing the Bach/Gounod version of "Ave Maria" with Chris Coutinho, an Indian-Kenyan singer and a devout Catholic. In November, Pope Francis was coming to Nairobi and Chris had been invited to perform in front of the pontiff. The pope's schedulers may have also likely been swayed by the fact that Chris would be accompanied by an orchestra that was from an informal settlement, something that was sure to pull the heartstrings of the pope.

In a country where twenty-eight percent of the population is Catholic—sixty thousand of them would be in attendance at the arena in Kasarani, and many of the rest would be watching the live television broadcast—it was also a great opportunity for even more exposure for the Ghetto Classics orchestra. For months, the GC kids practiced with Chris, who would come out to GC and bring along with him musicians playing the Indian flute, tabla drums, and the *nyatiti*, a Kenyan lyre traditionally played by the Luo people, which would be part of the performance.

Kepher had been chosen to conduct the orchestra, and since he had converted to Catholicism, the idea of performing in front of Pope Francis was a great thrill. On the day of the papal visit, Kepher had dressed in a black button-down shirt (including white cufflinks), a black vest, and a white bowtie. Meanwhile, the GC orchestra were dressed in their black "Ghetto Classics" T-shirts and seated in white plastic chairs. The day was blustery and cool, with many of the Maasai in the audience bundled up in their traditional bright red-and-blue wool *shuka* shawls, while others were in coats and knit caps. "I was nervous," Kepher said. "The wind was blowing and it opened my score to another page, but it taught me a lesson: nowadays I try to understand and cram the full piece in my head a little bit so then I can just glance at the score. But luckily I knew the song."

Such a pressurized, globally watched event was a great honor and experience for the orchestra and for Kepher, who throughout the performance had a stern face and looked every bit like a professional conductor with his white baton, because he had learned the importance of being able to wordlessly communicate with the orchestra when things didn't go as planned. "In rehearsal Chris couldn't hold the two bars, but on the day of the concert, he held a note for four bars," Kepher said. "But [the orchestra] understood me." As Kepher put his baton down, the crowd went wild, including invited dignitaries like President Uhru Kenyatta.

"I still remember, it was an amazing performance," he said, adding that the orchestra was directly in front of the pope so they could see his every reaction. "Chris hitting the notes in that big stadium—it sent chills down everyone's spine." Simon K. said that he glanced at Pope Francis, who looked pleased.

A month later, Kepher had barely come down from that high when he, along with forty-nine other GC members, including Celine and Erick, were invited to spend the week at the State House. President Kenyatta's wife, Margaret, had started a program called the Pupils Reward Scheme, where kids from across the country—usually students who were high achieving—got to learn all the inner workings of government. Students were briefed on the three arms of government, attended a cabinet meeting if there was one, and headed to the High Court to see a trial. The idea was that they were learning about their country and their government, as one day they might be the ones to change it from the inside.

President Kenyatta sometimes would pop by to meet the kids attending the program, which, as luck would have it, happened during the week the GC kids were there. They had preemptively brought their instruments just in case. "I said, 'Mr. President, your Excellency, and your Deputy, please stand up for the national anthem of the Republic of Kenya,'" Kepher said, laughing that he had told President Kenyatta what to do. "He told me he felt what I felt about the anthem. He didn't treat me as an official but as a buddy." Kepher must have made a strong impression on the president, because he was later awarded a scholarship from the Kenyatta Trust, the eponymous foundation that funds education for students from underprivileged backgrounds.

For Ghetto Classics, the year 2015 ended on a high note.

Seven

With his striking bright green eyes, a well-coiffed beard, and olive-skinned complexion, you'd be forgiven for mistaking Jorge Viladoms for a model. But while he has served as a brand ambassador for Swiss watchmakers Jaeger-Lacoultre and Rolex, he is best known as a concert pianist, professor, and philanthropist. Born in Durango, Mexico, in 1985, he only started playing piano as a fifteen-year-old after his father's untimely death. Music was, he has said, a way to drown out all the pain, confusion, and noise in his head. At eighteen he was accepted to the Lausanne Conservatory of Music in Switzerland—where Jorge later became a professor—and went on to complete a graduate degree from Hochschule der Künste Zürich (University of the Arts) as well. Jorge has performed in some of the world's greatest concert halls, and his first album, *From Latin America to Paris*, with the Bavarian Radio Symphony's principal cellist Lionel Cottet, was released in 2017.

Jorge always felt that music had saved him as a teenager and he believed that it could positively change the trajectory for other young people as well. So in 2012, he founded the Crescendo con la Musica Foundation, with its focus on giving free access to music for children living in poverty in Mexico. The pianist strongly felt that learning to play an instrument not only helped young people develop enthusiasm, imagination, and concentration, but it also gave them strong organizational skills and the opportunity to think critically and analytically. So when New York-based violinist Christopher Coritsidis reached out to Jorge out of the blue to ask him if he'd like to go with him to Nairobi in February 2016 to do some work with an orchestra called Ghetto Classics, Jorge was intrigued. He neither knew much about Chris—who got in touch with Jorge because of the philanthropic work he was doing in Mexico—nor the Kenyan slum orchestra. But since he'd never been to Africa and the project sounded like something that would appeal to him, he decided to go.

The musicians played three concerts in Nairobi, including one at the National Museum and another at the Tribe Hotel, where they met Elizabeth for the first time. She took them to Korogocho, and for Jorge it was a life changing experience. "I will never forget that day," he said. "It was hot, there were the kids on the street removing the trash. The crowds, the storks, the school, and the kids, it was all shocking." Though Jorge had obviously seen poverty in Mexico, what he saw in Korogocho was on another level altogether. "You sort of lose faith," he said.

But then the orchestra started playing, with Kepher on conducting duty. The musicians impressed Jorge, not because their sound was great (in fact, they sometimes were so off-key that it was a bit tedious to listen to), but the juxtaposition of playing such beautiful compositions with a toxic garbage dump just over the walls compelled him. "I was thinking, 'Where am I? What is happening here?'" he said with a laugh. After their rehearsal, Jorge spoke with some of the kids, who told him a bit about their backgrounds and he instantly knew he wanted to commit to helping GC. Jorge went to meet with Bob at Safaricom to talk about finding solutions and raising some funds. "What struck me most about where they play was the smell," he said. "I said to Bob, 'Why not build something away from the dump? A protection from all of that.'"

The foundation that Jorge had created in Mexico had funded a music program in a not-so-great neighborhood. "[It] is sort of a bubble where they can do whatever they want," he said. Jorge headed back to Switzerland not only determined to raise money to buy land for a center for GC outside of Korogocho, but he had also promised to help pay for the school fees for several boys. He had also been very taken with Kepher. "When I saw him first conduct, it was a shock," Jorge recalled of their first meeting at Korogocho. "I was impressed with his charisma, how he moved, the movement of his hands. And then Elizabeth told me his story, and how he learned to conduct on YouTube." Afterwards Jorge had a long talk with Kepher.

That spring Kepher had applied for the Mahler Conducting Competition, one of the most important music competitions in the world, held every three years in Bamberg, Germany, and open to anyone under the age of thirty-five. In 2004, Gustavo Dudamel won it decisively, and it's been seen as a stepping-stone for a successful international career ever since. In his sometimes charming, sometimes bombastic way, Kepher had applied online at the last minute, sending in the video of him conducting for Pope Francis. While he wasn't shortlisted for the prize, according to Kepher, the judges were so impressed with his backstory and his boldness that they invited him to Bamberg to be a special guest at the competition, and even paid for the trip. Kepher reached out to Jorge to tell him the good news and Jorge invited him to visit him in Lausanne afterwards so that he could sit in on conducting classes and speak with the faculty at the Conservatoire.

Kepher's experience in Bamberg was an incredible time for him. He not only got a chance to meet Gustav Mahler's granddaughter, Marina (who in 2006 won a six decades' long restitution battle with the Austrian government over an Edvard Munch painting that was owned by her grandfather), he also spent time with Maestro Jonathan Nott of the Bamberg Symphony Orchestra, who gave him private tutorials in the mornings. In Switzerland Kepher met with students at the Lausanne Conservatoire who were doing master's degrees in conducting, and he was even given the chance to direct the first movement of Sergei Prokofiev's *Romeo and Juliet*. He also had long discussions with students and faculty about applying to do an undergraduate degree in conducting at the school, which Jorge also encouraged. "He was staying with me for a few days and I was very impressed; he was up studying his scores, trying to be better, and everything he thought about was music," said Jorge. "One day we went for a walk around Lake Geneva and had an ice cream; it was a beautiful day. Then a boat passed by, and it made a sound, and the first thing he said was, 'What note is that?' His whole life is drawn to music."

While it was all a wonderful and exciting learning experience for Kepher, once he got back to Korogocho, Elizabeth, Levi, and others soon noticed that his experiences abroad had seemingly gone to his head. Kepher struggled coming back home and he lacked the social maturity and capacity to handle it well. He truly believed that he was going to be one of the world's great conductors. It was a lofty goal made all the more unrealistic because he had huge chunks of music theory missing from his education that would be integral for an international career in conducting. And while Elizabeth was eager to have him take advantage of the opportunities that might await him, saying, "I cannot stop anyone's trajectory; this is their life journey, and if that door is open then they should go through it," she and Levi also felt he had to be realistic in his dreams. Elizabeth also worried that it was partly her fault—that as the head of GC, she should have taken more precautions by tapering his expectations and being more attuned to something like this happening.

She asked Levi, who often handled many of the issues that popped up with the young men in GC, to talk with him. One of the pitfalls that they were worried about for Kepher (or in fact, any GC member who was given a similar chance) was that he had gotten so used to being treated specially at music events because of where he hailed from that he wasn't being held to the same standards as other musicians, at least at first. Kepher truly believed that he was better than he really was because people who were impressed with his backstory lauded him. He didn't have enough life experience to understand that what impressed people wasn't how he conducted but that he even was conducting at all.

"I had the same experience," Levi said "When I first played with an international orchestra in Italy, it was really nice and I had a good time. The second time, not as nice, and [the] third time, it was rubbish. And they stop looking at you like, 'This guy is from Africa; let's be nice.' People start to look at you as a conductor and they expect you to do your job."

And if Kepher really was serious about applying to school in Lausanne, he had a lot of catching up to do before he could be a competitive applicant. Being from the slum had, in a converse way, gotten him so far and that had opened up many musical doors, but Kepher had to learn that he couldn't rely on that as a fallback. "A year after the Westgate Mall terrorism incident, GC and KNYO were asked to perform at a commemoration," Levi recalled. "But what we did not tell the audience was that some of them were from GC. I told the orchestra later that while they had been given a leg up by Elizabeth coming from the situation that they did, they now had to perform like anyone else because that stops to matter at some point."

Levi felt that Kepher could go far if he put his mind to studying and also to acknowledging that he still had much to learn. GC would support him and "big him up" because what he had achieved with his drive and determination was impressive. "But it is your responsibility to put yourself in line and say, 'Actually, this is where I am realistically,'" Levi told Kepher. "Because if you lose sight of reality, then you are going to crash at some point, and when all the things dry away, then what you are holding up has got to be more content." Levi began tutoring Kepher on music theory.

Kepher wasn't the only GC musician Elizabeth was concerned about that year; Samwel, Precious, and Celine were all giving her cause to reassess her managing style and her mentoring relationship with the musicians.

Though she had a great affinity for a number of the kids that she had worked with over the years at Ghetto Classics, a few touched Elizabeth's heart, either because of their sad backstories or their proficiency as musicians and leaders within GC. Samwel had been one of those kids; even though he had developed a slick and tough aura which he carried around like a shield, he had promising talent and had become a good teacher to the younger kids. He also had big dreams and had told Elizabeth and Bob that he wanted to study aeronautical engineering in a university. "I loved physics and chemistry," Samwel said, "but my grades were not good."

Though he'd previously broken her trust over the school fees fiasco, since then he had been pretty much on the straight and narrow. As a member of SYO he'd gotten to know Bob as well, and the CEO told him that if he achieved a C+ or higher on his final exams, he would help Samwel with his university fees. "Bob was trying to get him into college and I was trying to get him an internship," Elizabeth recalled. "We were working our asses off to get him into school." In the end, he didn't get that C+, but he was able to doctor his grades to make it look as though he had. He then shared his false grades with Elizabeth and Bob, who were very pleased with what he said he had seemingly achieved. "After the results were announced, I was with that problem because I thought I would get a scholarship," he said. "I believed in myself, and the results came and I was like, 'What happened to me?'"

Samwel, who when he first joined GC had a nerdy air to him, had started to pick up a swagger around Korogocho after his false exam results. He was getting paid—well—by a short-term project funded by the World Bank to do cleanup in the slum. According to Elizabeth, Samwel was flush with money, "living large, getting drunk, and being a nuisance." He'd almost gotten in a fight with Kevin, one of his closest friends, and bragged to his GC peers, including Celine and a saxophonist named Joseph Omondi, that he was lying about his grades. "You're an idiot," he reportedly told Celine, who also had hoped to get some financial help for her schooling but also had not done well. "You could have lied like me."

Celine and Joseph told Elizabeth about the treachery, having heard a bit about Samwel's boasts, and Elizabeth was sent a screen grab with Samwel's grades that included an index number that served as his ID. "He had not changed that index number, but the contents of his grades changed," said Elizabeth, still angry from the memory. "Kenya is schizo because there is a phone number you can send your index number to. I sent his number to that, and his real grade came, and it was a D-." She forwarded the message back to Samwel without saying anything else in the text. He knew his game was up and he did not respond to the text. "That was when he started getting drunk," said Elizabeth. "So I told him he was not allowed if he was coming like that."

It was bad timing for Samwel because the money was running out from the World Bank project, and now that Elizabeth was refusing to give any financial support, he was struggling. "He really broke my heart over that one," Elizabeth said about the deceit. "I wonder if I did the right thing in supporting him during those years, or should I have weaned him off?" It was a question that she struggled with for years after; that in trying to help him, maybe she had in fact burdened him with the expectation that she would always be there to solve his problems and had prolonged his dependence and irresponsibility.

Bob and Levi were also disappointed. "Samwel wanted to be treated like a child long after he had grown up, and yet he kept coming back to Elizabeth, and she could not say no," said Levi. "He knew she had a soft spot for GC people, so even though he was no longer a teenager he was expecting her to help him. I said to her, 'No, no, no. All other twenty-something men in Kenya find themselves a job and sort themselves out.'"

A few months later, Samwel reached out to Elizabeth over text message, asking to speak to her and talk over what happened. It pained her—especially because he now had an infant daughter named Scarlet—but she ignored his messages. Bob had always told both Samwel and Celine that his door was always open to them and so when he contacted Bob to see him to ask for money for an investment in a small cybercafé, Bob took the meeting. "I told him that he had let people down and though people made mistakes, what was he going to do about it to set things right?" Bob recalled. "I said, 'I give you the time, don't say that people turn their back on you, there are many people who cannot get twenty minutes in my diary.'"

According to Samwel, Bob told him to come up with a proposal for the business and bring it to him. "So I came up with a work plan, went to his office, and he never showed up and I was like, 'Ugh, my God," he said. However, according to Kevin, Samwel was always late for things and that it was likely Bob had every intention to meet him but Samwel's tardiness meant he missed the meeting. For weeks on end he would text Bob's personal assistant every day to ask for a meeting but she, according to Samwel, never replied to him. "Deep in my heart, I knew what I did was wrong and I really regret it, I really miss the music," he said, admitting in 2017 that he still tried to get in touch with Bob and Elizabeth but they didn't return his texts and phone calls any more. In March 2017, he wrote on his Facebook page: "With..you..liz, i..know..i.would..have..gone..far, am..sorry..for..everything." When asked later about the text, Samwel, who admitted he was scavenging in the dump to make money for his family, mumbled sadly, "GC, I can say, it was like a family. And it was an opportunity place. That is the place to be."

Though Samwel's deception was very hurtful to Elizabeth, it was Precious who truly broke her heart.

Soon after taking Precious under her wing in 2015, the sixteen-year-old told Elizabeth that she pregnant. "I was raped," she said matter-of-factly when speaking on the library steps at St. John's in 2019. Elizabeth was heartsick for the girl and Precious told her that she wanted to stay in school but that she also wanted to have the baby. "And then my problem-solving skills kicked in and I said, 'Okay, we are going to do this,' and I was making phone calls," said Elizabeth. "And then the scariest thing, the thing that may haunt me, that I continue to question, is that I made such important life decisions for her."

Elizabeth wanted to see that Precious's pregnancy was as smooth as it could be under the tumultuous circumstances so she took her to the Nairobi Women's Hospital and found out she was twenty-three weeks pregnant. She asked Precious if she wanted to go back to Korogocho but Precious said no, so Elizabeth found a place for her to live until she had the baby in August 2015. "I took her out of a system that she knew and put her somewhere else, though she did ask me to," she ruminated, adding that over time, she began to understand that Precious had mental health issues, which often manifested itself in her lying. "I took her away from her life."

After she gave birth, Elizabeth arranged that her son, Stephen[4]—named after a St. John's priest who helped Precious get a burial plot for her mother, who according to Elizabeth had died from AIDS—would be taken care of in a children's home not far from Korogocho and that Precious could visit as often as she liked. Elizabeth also moved Precious in with Emily and her sister, Sharon, until she started boarding school in Kajiado, a region in the Rift Valley two hours away from Nairobi. At first, Precious did well in school, getting good grades. But the teen not only missed Stephen but also GC and Korogocho, and miles away in a rural boarding school, Precious

---

4   Not his real name

started to lose it. The headmistress told Elizabeth that sometimes Precious would wake up in the middle of the night screaming and would become violent. She was a very troubled young woman.

When she came home for school holidays in July 2016, she quickly transitioned back into GC but members noticed that she was often also hanging around with a crowd that was trouble. She also felt like she did not belong there anymore. On one hand, Precious knew what an opportunity she had been given by Elizabeth. If it had not been for her, Precious likely would have already dropped out of school and fallen into a life of hustling, her son permanently taken away from her. But she also couldn't stand the thought of going back to that boarding school, so far away from Korogocho and the life that she knew. So she made the decision to not go back, much to Elizabeth's despair. "I was feeling like they were laughing at me because I was not in school anymore," Precious said, her rich, coffee-brown eyes looking up at the sky. Making a clicking sound with her tongue, she pontificated, "They were talking about me and so I felt uncomfortable and stopped coming around to GC." However, Precious did go back to live with Emily, a situation that would soon turn treacherous.

Though violence was rarely far away from the lives of the young musicians—either at home or merely walking through Korogocho to school or practice—there was zero tolerance for it at GC, so Elizabeth was blindsided when she found out that Celine had struck one of the teenage musicians, Charity, before a Safaricom concert.

Born in Korogocho, Charity was the youngest child of her mother, Margaret Adhiambo, who also had older twin sons. When Charity was only two, her father left her mother. A tall, dignified woman with a respectable air who was very much involved in local Luo politics, Margaret was a teacher at St. John's School. Though Charity first secretly joined GC's dance troupe in 2014, where she would dance at baptisms and other church events, after a year she fessed up to her mom that she was spending her time at St. John's and told her she wanted to start playing an instrument. Margaret encouraged her daughter because it was a safe place for Charity to spend Sunday afternoons, and also, because of her meager salary, often they would run out of food by the weekend. "But at concerts they would serve us things to eat, so joining GC also helped me get my basic need, which is food," said Charity. "So it really makes my mom not worry about how I am eating. But I do wonder, how are my brothers going to take their food?"

The slap from Celine was a misunderstanding between the two teens over Celine's musical notebook. That day Charity had not gone to school, and knowing report cards were coming out, she had asked her friend Tracy Akinyi Ogutu, a sweet bashful clarinetist, to pick hers up. Wanting to read the card in private so the others wouldn't tease her, she slipped it into Celine's notebook. However, Celine, seeing Charity reading her notebook, flew into a rage, yelling at her about taking her things, and before Charity could explain herself, Celine hauled off and whacked her hard across the face. Everyone who witnessed it was shocked.

In tears, Charity ran to find her mother to tell her what had happened. Margaret was livid. There was already enough brutality that her daughter and her bandmates had to endure around Korogocho, but for the incident to have happened in an organization that she saw as a safe haven for her child was inexcusable. Margaret decided to head to Safaricom to confront Celine over the incident but before things could come to a head, Elizabeth intervened and calmed that situation down. Celine apologized but to her great embarrassment, the whole incident got back to Bob, who felt a special kinship to the young woman. Celine looked upon Bob as a role model. "I don't know why I did it," Celine confessed, very obviously mortified about the event. "Maybe I was angry, and I normally have this bad temper, but I try and control it. But it is hard."

For Elizabeth, the incident with Celine just reinforced that she needed to take some time away and reflect on what was not only happening overall in GC, but what her role was as a manager and mentor to many of the young people in the program. It also brought home to her that despite all the positives these kids were getting from being in GC, they also had been raised around bloodshed, trickery, and crime, and those aspects of their lives were always just as much there. Music couldn't simply erase all that.

The incidents with Samwel, Precious, and Celine throughout

2016 also brought to the fore issues that GC members had been gossiping about with each other for some time. It was that people like Celine—whom some members viewed as a mentor and others saw as a brownnoser—had gotten off lightly while others would have been punished more severely if they had done the same thing. That left some GC kids slightly bitter. Emily, for example, felt that while Elizabeth had much to be proud of in what she had done for so many kids over the years, it wasn't fair that some members seemed to get special treatment over others. It was starting to create hostility.

* * *

In August, Elizabeth travelled to Aspen, Colorado, to take part in the Aspen Institute's weeklong "Executive Seminar on Leadership, Values, and the Good Society," something she had been nominated to go on by a friend who worked for Oxfam and was in her "Sistas Chippin' In" *chama*, an informal cooperative society used to pool and invest savings by people in East Africa. The cost was almost prohibitive but her father, impressed that people like Condoleezza Rice, the former US secretary of state, was involved in the Institute, helped her fund the trip.

The leadership conference wasn't about boring power-point presentations. It was focused on conversations that looked critically at issues around self-leadership, testing values, and examining trade-offs that sometimes had to be made in order to run a successful organization. These three focuses were exactly what Elizabeth had been thinking a lot about. During the week, after doing some of the required readings, which included Plato and Herman Melville's *Billy Budd*, she would go for walks, sometimes on her own and sometimes with others. Her cohort included a surgeon, two men who worked for the CIA, a Norwegian shipping tycoon, and a banker from Switzerland. The fresh air of the mountains gave her the space she needed to reflect on where she wanted to take Ghetto Classics and the Art of Music Foundation.

Her time on maternity leave a few years before had shown a weakness in the Art of Music's organizational structure, and while she was the founder and figurehead, GC was not all about her anymore. Elizabeth understood that she suffered from "founder's fatigue,"—a burnout that happens as an organization started by one person grows and changes—in large part because she was constantly being asked to put out a thousand fires every week. When Ghetto Classics had started eight years before, it had been a passion-driven project, all guns blazing, but as it organically grew there had been no reflection on a long-term plan.

It was the same problem that many Sistema-inspired programs had found themselves in, and the reason that so many eventually shut down. "There is so much excitement and suddenness to the opportunity that they start revving up, and founders are usually unusual suspects who are starting these programs," said Eric Booth. "They are generally not seasoned managers, not seasoned entrepreneurs; they are going at it every waking moment and figuring it out as they go." The pressure on Elizabeth's shoulders—from the staff and the students to Safaricom's expectations to expand the GC program—was tremendous.

One day, her cohort members were putting together their presentation of Sophocles's *Antigone.* It was the required last project and groups could interpret it however they liked. Elizabeth's group was doing theirs based around the backdrop of *Dallas,* the 1980s American television show. She had an interesting conversation with one of the participants who worked in aerospace engineering in France. "He told me, 'In order to do more, you need to do less,'" she said. "And that really stuck with me."

His comment encapsulated something that her board had been telling her for years; that she needed to step away from the day-to-day and focus more on the long-term survival of the Art of Music Foundation programs, which now also included the Link Up project. Elizabeth also understood that she needed to be a more effective communicator with her staff because she often internalized problems and would not talk them out. "It can be very frustrating if you are on the other side and you do not know what is going on," Elizabeth admitted. "So if Levi is asking me if we are going to have a KNYO residential training, and we have no money in the bank account but

I believe in a miracle, I do not answer because I do not want to say 'no.' I know that Levi and the staff really struggled with that because I keep things on the inside."

Elizabeth also knew she had to take an emotional step back from the kids. In order to be an efficient leader, she had to have more distance, which was one of the reasons she had recently hired on Peter Kuria to be a full-time social worker for GC.

When she came back from Aspen, the Art of Music Foundation staff had their first team-building exercise at the Great Rift Valley Lodge in Naivasha, and the woman who was running it told Elizabeth that she had to tell her staff her story, so they could see what angle she was coming from. "She told me I had to make myself vulnerable to my staff," she said, mocking horror. "I was not on the bus on the way back home but one of the people on the bus said that they were grateful for that weekend because now they knew where they were going, and tomorrow I was not going to say, 'Okay we are done; it's closed.'"

It was, she said, a huge lesson for her in sharing and that even if she did not know the answer, it was okay to communicate that. "Elizabeth used to be that phone call about everything, but there is a bit of the organization now that has learned to be quite independent," said Levi. "So people are starting to settle in and dig into their own resources. For example, if I am in London and we need more batons, I'll get them. So we encourage that." In other words, the staff, and even the musicians themselves, were also learning to be more proactive on things and take more of an initiative. Elizabeth was sometimes able to take a back seat and watch things happen, which had not been the case in the past.

"She now has a strong administrative team and there is a system running," said Moses, reflecting on how things started to change once she came back from Aspen. "So it has moved from being personality driven to system driven in terms of the day-to-day running of things. She raises funds, and sometimes she takes a break, and things still run smoothly."

With her new leadership philosophy in place, and her staff, which included nine full-time employees as well as over twenty-five music tutors, feeling more emboldened to not have to run every little thing by her, she could focus on the upcoming Link Up concert at the end of October 2016.

Link Up had been a major opportunity because it not only gave more structure to teaching within GC for the newer members, it also allowed the program to expand beyond Korogocho. The program works by sending the curriculum and resources that are used throughout the school year to teach beginners the early steps in music theory. Link Up materials also include instructions for how the final show should run, including using a local orchestra—for Link Up Kenya, it was KNYO—to help be the backbone of the musical showcase. One of the cornerstones of the project was that it should be adapted into the local milieu, so Elizabeth got six local schools—some in Korogocho and some in places like Mukuru Kwa Ruben, another slum in Nairobi—on board so that each week, over three hundred children in their own classrooms were all learning the same material and music on their recorders. Link Up was about teaching the basic principles of being in an orchestra. "When they rehearse for their final show with KNYO, when the orchestra tunes, they tune the kids too," said Elizabeth. "The feeling is that of being in a real orchestra; there is a whole script and they tell you how to run the concert."

For the October showcase, the kids were working on a program called "Orchestra Moves," focused on movement in music and examining the principles of how music speeds up and slows down. They played "Habanera," a can-can song and a Brazilian dance tune from *Carmen*. Even before the concert happened—which included the then US ambassador, Robert F. Godec, in attendance—Bob hoped that the Link Up program could be expanded to schools in Mombasa in 2017. Elizabeth, recharged since her time in Aspen and the success of the parents' concert that September, agreed to start looking into branching out the program to the Swahili coast. And the Link Up concert was seen as a resounding success.

But just the next day, what Elizabeth, Simon K., Levi, Kevin, and everyone else had always feared would happen, did. St. John's caught on fire.

Eight

Celine and Martha Aluoch Awura, a violinist who joined GC in 2015, had had their fair share of disagreements, mostly teenage girl stuff. But on October 24, 2016—for that day at least—all those other things went out the window. Literally.

The two women stood hugging each other, united and crying as they watched the building burn where GC had their offices and kept some instruments, including a piano. "That day there was big smoke in Korogocho," Celine remembered. "I was on my way to St. John's and I ran into some of my friends who said that the fire at the dumping site had spread up to our music room." They also told her that some of the people who worked at the dump site had started the fire because there was a lot of paper that had been dumped that day and they wanted to clear the area for more garbage. Some of the burning paper had wafted and waned over to St. John's, landing on the roof and starting the blaze. Celine took off at a quick pace towards St. John's and when she got through the gates a little after 3:00 p.m., what she witnessed was bedlam.

David Six, a pianist from Austria, had come that day to St. John's to do a master class with the kids, and he, along with a number of the GC members who were in attendance, and Elizabeth were running in and out of the administrative building, carrying instruments, music stands, African drums, and desks. "The smoke was so bad," Martha recalled, "we had to run in and grab what instruments we could, it was so chaotic." Celine sprinted into the cement building as well, up the cracked, cream-colored stairs that permanently stunk of urine, past the music room on the left, and down the smoky hall to the GC offices, which faced the amphitheater and school buildings about one hundred meters away.

Running into the room—its walls decorated with inspirational music quotes like "Music begins where the possibilities of language end"—she helped the others with the piano, getting it down the stairs to safety. (Later, David, who seemed overwhelmed by the chaos, kept asking Elizabeth if he could play the piano, which they had gently abandoned on the basketball court, to "make everyone feel better.") The books and music, however, weren't as lucky. They were ruined and yellow from the smoke and flames. It was getting too dangerous for anyone to go back into the building, and so all the kids and GC staff were ordered to go onto the football pitch. Celine and Martha sobbed together, frightened that the entire building was going to burn down, and with it, GC as well.

Luckily, a fire truck arrived with water on board (which wasn't always the case) and they were able to put out the blaze before there was too much damage. Plus, "by God's grace it started raining and that helped to put out the fire," Martha said. A few men who worked at the dump site tried to climb over the gates of St. John's. "Some of them wanted to help and some of them wanted to take advantage of the situation," Celine said, adding that the men knew GC had instruments and probably other valuables that they could loot amidst all the confusion. The police arrived and handcuffed the young men, planning to arrest them for trespassing.

But the librarian from St. John's walked over to the police, who, according to Martha, begged them: "Don't arrest them, because if you do, it will mean more trouble for us." The police relented, letting the men go with a strict warning, and things started to calm down. "It was really sad," Celine said. "We had a month without music because the smoke was too much." Even after GC opened again in November, that rancid smell of the fire continued to permeate in the rooms for over a year.

While the fire and its aftermath were traumatizing for the Ghetto Classics kids, tutors, and the overall GC community, conversely what it helped reinforce was that despite the minute internal dramas that flared up from time to time, GC members had truly become a family that united during the tough times. "Ghetto Classics is like my second family because we help each other," said Charity. "We make each other feel better, and that is very important to me." Her mother, Margaret, agreed, saying that GC was a special place. "It is like a home to these children; they can share," she said. "It's filled with very good people who care. People who are thieves, those kids will not be that. They have education and love."

Kevin, when creating a WhatsApp group for GC members who had smartphones so they could more easily communicate, didn't hesitate on what to name the group: Ghetto Classics Family. "It is only at home that you get advice, it is only at home that you get refuge, it is only at home that you can get care, it is only at home that you get security," Kevin said when trying to define why many members felt a special kinship to GC. "There are issues of discipline, lack of cooperation sometimes among the kids, lack of honesty sometimes also from the kids, but that is what most families experience, and we experience certain challenges as this family faster than some other families. Even challenges within the community, with the smoke, the security, but we are a family, and we are struggling to push forward." For someone like Kevin, who had had a traumatic early start in life, Ghetto Classics filled an enormous gap and every time he spoke of it, his whole face would light up.

For most of the musicians and staff, there was also a sense of ownership that had developed over the years that GC was not something that one merely joined, but it was something one became. "Everybody feels 'Ghetto Classics is mine' on a personal level," Kevin reflected after the fire. "I think everyone is ready to take any responsibility, and this goes down even to the kids. I have even heard kids who will try to scorn people who are talking bad about GC saying, 'You don't know what you are talking about.'" Those feelings of ownership also created commitment and confidence; things that weren't inherently being taught but were positive byproducts of the program.

Members felt they had a vested interest in how the organization was run, and projects that they were keen to see be developed, from Simon M.'s idea for the parents' concert to the creation of a student council (implemented by Simon K.), one for the primary school kids and one for secondary school members. Simon M. and Tracy became the representatives for the older kids and met every few weeks with Simon K. to discuss different issues and ideas that had come up through conversations and situations. One of the things that they had formulated was a substantial list of rules and regulations that GC members had to adhere to, like: "Strictly use the instrument registered under your name," and "No taking any stationaries from the office without permission." The rules, printed on A4 paper, were taped up in the GC offices for all to see.

But the musicians weren't just inspired to create changes within GC; some had also come to see, in part through their time in the program and their exposure to a broader outside world—which included not just meeting internationally renowned musicians, top diplomats, dignitaries, academics, filmmakers, and development professionals, but also getting the chance to travel across the country and abroad—that they could also help make changes within the wider Korogocho community as well.

For Stephen Ayoro, the fire became a call to arms. The GC trumpeter, who had joined the program in 2011 and became a tutor a year later, had witnessed firsthand how people-led initiatives could inspire change within the community. When the fire happened that October, he was in the midst of doing a degree in agriculture at the University of Nairobi. From his studies—and from growing up around Korogocho—he knew that toxic and dangerous chemicals from the dump were seeping into the soil. The fire had also brought home how dangerous the overall dump site situation was, not only to the slum in terms of the massive fire hazard, but also for the thousands of people who worked in the slum every day. He read with disgust stories from Addis Ababa, Ethiopia, just a few short months after the GC fire, where in March 2017 over one hundred people had been buried alive in the Reppi dump during a landslide of garbage. He worried the same could happen in Nairobi.

Stephen and community activist Japeth Ogola (who was married to Martha's sister) spent a lot of time talking about what could be done because there was seemingly no movement to close the illegal dump on the border of St. John's. Japeth had been asked a few years before by UN Environment to give a presentation about how the dump was affecting the lives of people within the Korogocho community, and he passed his research materials onto Stephen. It was a dangerous endeavor to be seen as getting too involved with closing the dump because of the powerful overlords—some rumored to be city council members and top Nairobi politicians—who made money from the dump site. So fighting against them would have to be a careful, nuanced dance. Japeth, who years ago had inspired Simon K. to become a community activist, remembered that there had been a Twitter hashtag—#stopdumpingdeathonus—that had been created a few years before to pressure officials over the Dandora dump, so he and Stephen decided to recycle it, launching an online campaign to draw attention to the situation. With 2017 being an election year, it was a great time to get people's attention.

The fire also helped reinforce the fact that there was an entire ecosystem around GC, filled with international musicians, teachers, academics, volunteers, and diplomats who were dedicated to supporting the program in any way they could. While a number of musicians, like Arun Ghosh, Salif Keita, and Branford Marsalis (who after meeting the GC members in 2016 donated reeds for clarinets and saxophones), were touched by what was happening in Korogocho, they kept only loose contact. But others, like Jef Neve, Grammy Award-winning saxophonist Kirk Whalum, Stephanie Schiller, and Jorge, who had come back in August for a second concert to raise money for GC, after hearing about the fire were even more determined to see what they could do to continue to support the program.

For someone like Emily, the budding journalist who was keen to make changes within her community, the opportunity to network with the GC ecosystem turned out to be just as important to her as learning the violin. Along with her cute pixie nose and a quick rat-a-tat-tat laugh, Emily also had a wicked sense of humor, was fiercely independent, intelligent, well-spoken, and had moxie in droves. Her skill set included being able to quickly read and assess situations. With the networking instinct a strong part of her nature, Emily soon figured after she joined GC that the program was not only a place where for a few hours every Sunday she could get away from her problems and learn an instrument, but she might also be able to reap the advantages of being part of a program that was getting increasing attention both in Kenya and abroad.

And while Emily had a flair for the dramatic, she also was always brutally honest about her feelings towards GC. She never sugarcoated how things were and was often highly critical of how Elizabeth was running things. But she also loved her friends from GC and the experiences she'd had as a member, though at times she also took advantage of her affiliation with the orchestra. For example, much to the chagrin and consternation of Wamocho, she showed up for a highly anticipated—and much-rehearsed—concert in front of a well-to-do international audience in April 2019 having skipped all the practices. Rightly so, Wamocho told her she could not stay.

Born in 1992, Emily was somewhat unique among many of her GC colleagues because she was born in a hospital and her birth was registered. Her father, originally from Uganda, had wanted a son (he already had two daughters), and so her birth was a disappointment. Emily's arrival heralded the end of her parents' marriage, and her father soon left her mother for another woman. With no other options available to her, Emily's mother moved with her baby daughter to Korogocho while the older girls stayed with their father, who soon took another wife and had another daughter.

A bright and vivacious student, Emily attended primary school until class seven, but that year, when she was thirteen, she was forced to drop out because of the fees. Her mother had remarried and had two more children with her stepfather, whose last name Emily had taken. But he had refused to pay the money for her schooling and though Emily's mom scrambled to make money by selling fish on the streets of the slum, the paltry amount she made would not cover the costs. She said her stepfather was also violent towards her and he was unhappy that he was paying the way for another man's child.

All these ingredients were part of the recipe that made Emily's home life unbearable. So Emily ran away from the trauma to stay with an aunt and went to the Boma Rescue Center.

After a year at Boma, Emily went back to school, and while she was happy to be there—and her stepfather eventually left her alone—it was often very hard going because girls were the targets of sexual harassment, rape, and overall abuse. "Even inside the gates of my school, I was not free from the violence that permeates Korogocho," described Emily. "A number of students were from rehabilitation centers like the one I had been in, and there were often incidents of fighting, teachers being threatened by pupils, and some kids even carried guns. But I had friends in school and we shared a love of books and we competed to be the top of the class against the boys."

After graduating from secondary school in 2009, Emily did a theology course, worked odd jobs, was involved in her church choir, and learned taekwondo. In 2015, the same year she joined GC, she took a course in filmmaking and photography with K. Media, a local NGO teaching young people from various slums across Nairobi the power of storytelling. Emily, deciding this was her calling, soon got small paying jobs with two other social projects that promoted citizen journalism. Emily was especially interested in female empowerment and ending violence against women, due in large part to what had happened within her own family. Emily had also always loved music and she was intrigued by what was going on over at St. John's. And though as a twenty-three-year-old she was one of the older members when she joined—while mostly focused on youth, GC has always been open to anyone in the community—she never felt that she was not wanted or included because of her age. "That is one thing I really appreciated about GC, because I had been locked out of so many other things that I wanted to do," she stated. "So with GC I was very lucky."

Though she originally wanted to learn piano, she was moved in the direction of the violin and Kepher gave her private music theory lessons because she was so hungry to learn. "My musical background is in church, singing, but nothing technical like sight-reading, so I learned all that in GC," she said. "I have learned to play the violin and it has not only helped restore inner peace in me, but it also has presented me with different platforms to meet new people from all across the globe who come to mentor our music." What Emily also liked about being a part of GC was that she felt that, aside from the music, the program also emphasized something that had seemingly been forgotten by many in her community—a sense that people had the power and the ability to change their own lives and the environs where they lived in.

Emily was keen to one day open an arts center that promoted community empowerment through song, dance, and photography, and partly because of her drive and ambition, Elizabeth had hoped that Emily's positivity could be a good influence on Precious. She and her sister Sharon no longer lived in Korogocho, but in another slum that was about a twenty-minute walk away, so the idea was that taking Precious physically away from her surroundings could help her stay away from trouble and continue with her schooling.

But Emily wasn't always at home—she was also working part-time as an overnight nanny for a UN diplomat—and so Precious would often sneak back to Korogocho, sometimes not coming back until after 10:00 p.m. Some evenings, Precious wouldn't come home at all, and Sharon, concerned, would call Emily; the sisters speculated that Precious was dealing drugs, as she had gotten together with a gang leader who was trouble. "I thought she would one day change," Emily said, "because I kept talking to her and giving her the example of my sister, Iriene." (Her sister had been gang raped and contracted AIDS from one of her rapists. She gave birth to a daughter who was conceived during the rape. Iriene later died from AIDS.)

According to Emily, things came to a head in early 2017, when Precious started bringing sketchy men back to the studio flat when Emily was not there but her younger sister was. One Saturday evening, after not being home for two days, Precious tried to come into the flat, but Sharon, who was frightened, refused to let her in. Precious left but came back in the early hours of Sunday morning with two men, one of whom pulled a knife on Sharon. "I left work very early to come back home when my sister phoned me up," Emily recalled. "It was a real shock; this issue of the knife really pissed me off." Luckily a neighbor was able to intervene and no one was hurt. Emily screamed at Precious to get out, and she disappeared for several months. (Precious's account differed vastly, and she blamed Emily for spreading stories around Ghetto Classics that she was a bad person.)

"Many stories have come out," Elizabeth said, "and maybe I do not want to know the truth." Plus, Elizabeth had too many other things to focus on in the early part of 2017, including getting the Mombasa program up and running.

* * *

After the jazz festival with Arun Ghosh and David Sanborn
finished on Sunday, Elizabeth took off with Wanjiku for a few days to the coast. She had a chance to breathe in the saltwater air, lazily walk on the beach, and play in the smooth sand with her daughter, who at almost four had a strong and vivacious personality much like her own. The Link Up Mombasa program had started only a month before and was being run by Paul Sitnam, a tall, stout, bespectacled former GC trumpet tutor who had also been one of the Link Up teachers in Nairobi in 2016. He'd grown up in the Kenyan capital and had attended the Nairobi School, where he was involved in the music program and had gotten to know Moses. Elizabeth had been impressed with Paul's dedication and approached him about starting Link Up in Mombasa. He was interested and since his aunt lived in Mombasa, there wouldn't be an issue of him finding somewhere to live.

So on the following Tuesday after the festival in February 2017, Elizabeth and Safaricom's sponsorship manager, Mishi Wambiji, picked up Paul on the way to a car ferry, which would take them to the first Link Up school. Dressed in a long, loose seersucker shirt and black trousers, Paul made small talk in the car, explaining that because there was a drought happening along the coast, and the city felt like being inside a furnace on full blast, he'd found flowing tops kept him cool in the stifling classrooms and as he commuted to the four Link Up schools that were located in Mombasa's four districts. The city was made up of three peninsulas and an island nestled along the Indian Ocean with a total population of 1.5 million inhabitants.

Driving through the city filled with tourist shops often run by sales clerks pretending to be Maasai, market stalls spilling over with freshly caught fish and juicy produce, and brightly painted mosques in light greens, mustard yellows, and sea-foam blues, Paul talked about how as far back as the twelfth century, Mombasa had been a prosperous trading seaport. Kenya's second largest city had a rich and textured heritage that seamlessly weaved not only Islamic and Indian influences, but also traditions picked up under both Portuguese and British colonial rule. For years the city had been a popular gateway for tourism along the Swahili coast for Kenyans and Europeans alike, but Mombasa also had recently gained an international reputation as a breeding ground for the regional terrorism of fundamentalist group Al Shabaab.

Arriving at Likoni Primary School, the headmaster warmly greeted the group by saying how much the kids liked the program. "So far, so good," he said with a jovial chuckle, leading them down a recently swept dirt path to a white-and-blue building where the children had their weekly Link Up lessons. Merry young schoolgirls, dressed in royal-blue skirts, collared, bright white shirts, and white hijabs stood under the trees for shade, whispering and smiling and shyly waving to Paul as they entered the room, where the wooden music stands were neatly stacked in the corner. The headmaster said they'd love to have even more classes but Elizabeth explained that at this point they didn't yet have enough resources to hire more teachers. It was a common refrain she would have to repeat throughout the day at the other three schools.

Taking a ferry back to the mainland, by the time they arrived midday at the Khadija Primary School across town, it was sizzling and Elizabeth's and Paul's glasses steamed as they stepped out of the air-conditioned van.

One of the students, Hadiqa, dressed in a light-blue dress and white hijab, ran up to Paul as he got out of the vehicle and stood under some large, cooling fronds of the palm trees. "Do we have music today?" she asked him, excitedly. "No," he replied with a brief smile as several other girls appeared, diving under the trees to shade themselves. Hadiqa, who had a long, mischievous face, looked at him quizzically. With attitude, she curtly replied, "Yes, but teacher, you are here."

As Elizabeth walked over to be introduced to the teacher charged with helping organize the class, Paul explained that at Khadija, it was only the troubled kids who were enrolled in the program. Upon introduction, the female teacher, dripping so much with sweat that she kept repeatedly wiping her face with a moist plaid handkerchief, said that even though the classes had started only a few weeks before, she could already notice a positive difference in the thirty or so children in the program. The music students, who were on lunch break and had quickly gathered around when they saw Paul, first sang a pleasant, if staid, rendition of "Do, Re, Mi" before quickly transitioning into "Salome," a saucy song by popular Tanzanian singer Diamond Platinumz. The lyrics were slightly risqué for primary school kids, but the visitors laughed and figured that at least it showed they were excited for music.

After lunch and a visit to the third school, where Paul gave a recorder lesson and some of the girls performed a rousing song outside about the importance of staying in school and getting an education (and where Elizabeth received yet another request to have more Link Up classes), the group ended the day at the Mikindani Primary School. They met with the engaging head teacher, Susan Nyanga, who told Elizabeth in a conspiratorial tone that she was annoyed that the Kenyan government had cut subsidies to teach music in school. Susan then asked Elizabeth if the teachers could also sit in on the Link Up classes, because she realized that resources were limited and if her teachers were trained, they could sometimes help lead the class if Paul or his assistant were ever late.

"When something is good," Susan said, smiling as she aired out her light-green and orange swirled shirt in the sweltering school hallway, "people work for it."

St. John's rehearsal, date unknown
(courtesy of author)

**The very first instruments received by Ghetto Classics, bought
with a grant by the Goethe-Institut; from left, in front row,
Joseph Omondi (blowing saxophone), Stephen Ayoro in the
middle holding a trumpet and looking at camera, and Simon
Kariuki Ndungu, far right; directly behind him, Brian Kepher,
and to left, Samwel Otieno; October 9, 2011**
(Courtesy of Elizabeth Njoroge)

**Branford Marsalis jamming with Erick Ochieng
and Celine Akumu, 2016**

(courtesy of Elizabeth Njoroge)

**Simon Kariuki Ndungu teaching at St. John's,
September 2016**

(courtesy of author)

Kevin Obara and Elizabeth Njoroge at St John's, February 2017

(courtesy of author)

Simon Mungai, February 2017

(courtesy of author)

Lewinsky Atieno, Martha Aluoch, and Emily Onyango *(left to right)* at JazzFest in 2017

(courtesy of author)

Schoolchildren having music lesson in Mombasa, February 2017

(courtesy of author)

Jorge Viladoms with Teddy Otieno, date unknown

(courtesy of Elizabeth Njoroge)

Tracy Akinyi, Celine Akumu, Lewinsky Atieno, and David Mwenje, clarinet practice at St. John's, September 2017

(courtesy of author)

**Musicians outside after new garden is opened; note the
Ngomongo illegal dump site in the distance, April 2018**

(courtesy of Stephanie Schiller)

Violin lessons at St. John's, May 2018

(courtesy of author)

Woman scavenging in Dandora dump site, May 2019

(courtesy of author)

Marabou storks in the Dandora dump, May 2019
(courtesy of author)

Several GC musicians, including Erick Ochieng (second from left) and Simon Kariuki Ndungu (next to drummer) perform in Nairobi for Belgium's Queen Mathilde and daughter Princess Elisabeth, June 2019
(Courtesy of Elizabeth Njoroge)

Kirk Whalum with Joseph Omondi *(left)*, **date unknown**
(courtesy of Elizabeth Njoroge)

**President Barack Obama listening to the GC musicians playing
at Kempinski Hotel, Nairobi; Michael Joseph, the former CEO of
Safaricom, is to the left of President Obama (in a tie); summer 2018**

(courtesy of Giants of Africa/Gina Din Group)

**A skeleton rehearsal in Wroclaw—Benjamin Wamocho
is at the conductor's podium, summer 2018**

(courtesy of Jimek and Emalka Ziabska)

**Charity Akinyi and Manolo practicing percussion,
Wroclaw, summer 2018**

(courtesy of Jimek and Emalka Ziabska)

**GC musicians after performance in Wroclaw; at far left,
Benjamin Wamocho (in hat), at left, Chris Szymczak (kneeling),
in second row, Elizabeth (kneeling with glasses), and Jimek
(lying in front); summer 2018**

(courtesy of Jimek and Emalka Ziabska)

**Twins Teddy and Lamek Otieno with
Jimek and Peter Kariuki (holding
violin), practicing in Wroclaw, Poland,
summer 2018**

(courtesy of Jimek and Emalka Ziabska)

**Kevin Obara in Hamburg,
Germany, with Michael
Danner of Brasserie
Hamburg, June 2019**

(courtesy of author)

Jorge, Stephen Kamau, and Elizabeth, after Kamau was given his cello, Lausanne, Switzerland, January 2020

(courtesy of Jorge Viladoms)

**Kamau with his new cello, playing in
Lausanne, January 2020**

(courtesy of Alexia Linn)

Performing in Lausanne, Lewinsky Atieno *(far right)* **and Tracy Akinyi next to her, January 2020**

(courtesy of Alexia Linn)

Simon Kariuki Ndungu and Teddy Otieno in London with the author's dog, November 2022

(courtesy of author)

Nine

Posh East Hampton, New York, was figuratively and literally about as far away from Korogocho as Teddy and Kamau could have found themselves. The resort town on Long Island is filled with massive clapboard mansions and upscale organic farm stands selling fresh sweet corn and local tomatoes that are bright red, ripe, and bursting with flavorful tang. There are stylish boutiques, many of which are the slick summer outposts of favorite Manhattan haunts where wealthy Upper East Siders love to drop cash, and posh gyms that offer everything from hip-hop spin classes to bespoke personal training regimes with celebrity fitness gurus. Domestic goddess Martha Stewart, comedian Jerry Seinfeld, rock star Jon Bon Jovi, and fashion designer Donna Karan all have homes near town, and what people are seen wearing while swimming at Main Beach in the afternoon is as important as what is carefully thrown on for dinner at The 1770 House restaurant in the evening. For those looking to escape the heat, the people, the noise, the pollution, and the multiculturalism of New York City, look no further than East Hampton—though the social scene seems just as intense.

It was August 2017, and Kamau and Teddy were spending their second summer in the resort town at the International Music Sessions (IMS) camp, a two-week program helping classically trained teens advance their musicianship. There were almost thirty students, who were both local Hamptons summer kids and children from countries like the Democratic Republic of Congo, Mexico, and Vietnam, many of whom had little access back home to things like one-on-one tutorials or personalized music theory classes.

IMS, founded in 2012 by New York-based classical pianist Theresa Kim, was begun in part to help create engagement between artists and students from various walks of life, and it offered two-year camp scholarships. What the two GC musicians liked most about East Hampton, aside from getting to spend the day playing music at St. Luke's Church, with its lovely wooden interiors and quiet, airy practice rooms filled with bookshelves and pianos, was they could ride bikes to the beach, hang out with other kids, and eat as much ice cream as their bellies could handle. What Kamau and Teddy didn't realize was just how precariously close they had both been to not going back for that second summer.

Already a shy boy who had trouble making eye contact with adults and who lived somewhat in the shadow of his more engaging identical twin brother Lamek, for Teddy coming back to Korogocho had proved almost traumatizing for him. "Teddy is more introspective and he does not waste energy on too much other stuff; he is driven in a very quiet, steady way," Elizabeth said. "Kamau teaches the other kids, helping them learn, but Teddy does not do that; he does not share." His homecoming was a lot for the sensitive boy to take on board, and Elizabeth pondered whether it would be good for his mental state to let him go back to East Hampton in the summer of 2017, just to then have another very tough reentry to slum life.

Teddy's parents had of course also noticed that their son had found it difficult to be back home. Alloyce, a casual laborer and welder, and Phelister, who sold kale in a market stall, were proud of their sons, seeing that music had certainly changed the twins' lives for the better. And while Teddy had seemed to thrive during his time at IMS—his parents and brother Skyped a few times with him, and Teddy excitably told them all about what he was up to—Alloyce did admit that his son had had a tough time when he came back from America, having become so ill with a fever that he had to be taken to the hospital for injections. "He was not relaxed when he came home," his father said, sitting on the family's soft, brown sofa in their tidy home in Lucky Summer, where professional black-and-white individual photographs of both boys playing their respective instruments hung on the wall above. Teddy agreed, saying that it had been a very arduous time and that at first he had not wanted to come back home. "It was really hard that first day; it seemed like everything had changed," he said. "I had a hangover for a week, like, 'What is happening?'"

A lot of that was because he felt that life in Korogocho and the surrounding slums was nasty. "The gangs, they terrorize you, you cannot sleep at night," he said. "People climb on rooftops, they run all over while the police chase them." Teddy said he and his twin avoided joining the gangs—some made up of former schoolmates who had dropped out and become gunrunners—by saying they had to practice their music and didn't have time for much else. "But I tell them, 'You can come and join us,'" he said. "Plus my dad warned me that if I ever joined a gang, I cannot step foot inside his house."

Alloyce figured that his sons may have gotten their music skills from Phelister, who sang in a choir as a schoolgirl, and seeing his boys perform both at the National Theater and at the Boma Rescue Center had been a privilege. "I could not believe that those were my sons," he proudly said as he offered some chai tea. "If I had a video of those performances, I would watch it over and over on the television." He also felt that both boys' lives had improved once they joined GC. "There have been a lot of achievements we have seen from Teddy and Lamek since they got into music; they have become our music teachers," he said. "Academically they have improved a lot and their respect and behavior is much better." Teddy told his parents that he wanted to study medicine in the US, and that once he was settled there, he would bring the whole family over. "He made us proud, the whole family," his father said, adding that it meant a lot to them that on Teddy's first trip to America, the president at the time, Barack Obama, was half-Kenyan.

Meanwhile, Kamau, who like Teddy was also a member of SYO and KNYO, had come back to Korogocho from East Hampton in August of 2016 full of life, excited to tell his friends about what he had learned both about music and America. However, over the course of the year he started to develop an increasingly boastful attitude. The tall and nimble sixteen-year-old with high cheekbones and expressive wide eyes, whose robust cello often seemed to engulf him as he steadied the instrument in front of him, exuded both a maturity hidden behind a sweet but serious face, and a swagger of someone who seemed fearless. Elizabeth, at first pleased that he had come back enthused to show his fellow GC musicians all that he had picked up while in East Hampton, noticed over the year that he was increasingly acting up, and it worried her. "He started being naughty, getting into trouble with Simon [K.], and he was testing his boundaries," Elizabeth said. "And I told him, 'Kamau, want to go to the States? Then come back into line.' He was like, '*Ai-yi*, okay.' He is not a bad kid."

It had taken a lot of effort to get Kamau to IMS in the first place, in part because he had no birth certificate and that meant no access to a passport or a visa. Plus, his father was not in the picture much at all, but the US Embassy required that both parents, if alive, had to sign his paperwork since he was a minor. "I told his mother, 'I don't care where he is, if he's alive you bring him,'" Elizabeth recounted with a deep laugh. His mother, Jane Wangari Nginge—a round woman who eked out a living selling a local dish made of maize and beans, called *githeri*—with her always-present hearty laugh replied: "Oh, shit, you are kidding?" But Jane was able to strong-arm him in the end, and they went, along with Teddy's parents and Elizabeth, to the US Embassy for an interview and paperwork.

Jane was excited and proud that her elder boy (her younger boy, Samwel, was a percussionist in GC) was going on such an exciting adventure. "We always see planes fly over in the sky but I had never been to the airport," Jane recalled. "I was so proud that night because my son was going to be up in that silver tube and I just could not believe it. When we talked later, I asked him, 'What does it feel like when the plane goes up in the sky?'" After Elizabeth's threat that he wouldn't get to go back to IMS and his mother wouldn't get to think about him being up amongst birds again, Kamau's attitude changed—quickly.

Kamau did admit that he found it hard to go back home after IMS camp ended, and after what she had witnessed with Kepher, Elizabeth did have a much greater understanding that coming back to life in Korogocho was a tough transition.

On one hand he was proud to be from there—"It is where I live, it is where I am from"—but seeing how life could also be so much less complicated and hard made it a grim adjustment in the teen's mind. But there was never any question that Kamau, unlike Teddy, wanted to come back and make Korogocho a better place. "I would teach street kids and help them change their lives," he said fervently. "I would go back to Korogocho to help other people, because I was also helped."

Though Kamau lived with his mother, he used to run around with street children, many of whom would go daily into the dump to scavenge for plastic bottles and glass. "I would spend time with them because they were my friends," he said. "Nowadays I do not interact with them because I have changed my life; you cannot compare them to me right now." It was with one of his street friends that in 2014 he went to St. John's to watch some of the kids play football. "And I heard something, a sound I could not put my finger on and I was like, 'This is very good,'" he recalled, using his charmingly quirky way with words. For Kamau, GC also became a lifeline for his education, with the Art of Music Foundation paying his school fees. "Most of the girls drop out of school because of lack of money, then they get pregnant and have babies, and the boys, also because of school fees, they drop out and start to be criminals, you see," Kamau said. "When you wake up, it is not like in East Hampton, where you hear birds chirping and they are so melodious. The first thing in the morning you hear in Korogocho is someone being [robbed] or beaten."

In the end, Elizabeth relented and decided to send both boys back to East Hampton for the camp, in part because she figured it was safer than being in Kenya during the presidential elections that were scheduled for August 2017.

Though it was a stiflingly humid August day in East Hampton, Teddy was dressed in a thick black sweatshirt, a red T-shirt underneath, and dark jeans as he was taking his air-conditioned one-on-one lesson with his tutor, Jason Sugata, a horn player who regularly performed in Broadway musicals and appeared on stage with artists, including Jay-Z, Tony Bennett, and Lady Gaga. "You need to play with energy," Jason, dressed in the more appropriate summer attire of shorts and a button-down short-sleeve shirt, told Teddy. "I think you need to play it more musically, as if you are singing this." Teddy looked at him with intense concentration, nodded, and then started blowing in his tuba, keeping the beat by tapping his red-laced black sneakers on the floor. Jason, he felt, had been a great tutor and Teddy found that he had learned much from him over the past two summers.

Teddy, Jason said after the teenager played a few bars, had improved by leaps and bounds from his time last summer at IMS.

Two rooms away, Kamau, wearing black shorts, flip-flops, and a long-sleeved red-and-blue paisley button-down shirt with a camouflage vest, was getting a cello lesson from Jia Kim, a Korean-born, Juilliard-trained musician. "What am I counting? What are my beats?" Jia asked, leaning over his music stand and pointing to the sheet music. "You have to decide before we start if you are going to count in quarter or eighth notes. You want to do one, and two, and three." He picked up his bow and started again as she snapped her fingers along to the notes. Jia then asked Kamau how he read the music, and when he said he read each note as he played it, she stopped him. "I want you, when you look at the music, I want your eyes to go three notes ahead of what you are actually playing," she said, looking at him intensely while she spoke. "So your eyes are always a little bit ahead of your hands." Kamau tried again; this time the music coming from his cello was smoother and more fluid.

After his practice with Jia, Kamau talked about the imminent presidential elections back in Kenya and the tensions they were causing in his community. Since the violence of the 2007 elections, Kenyan presidential elections were always tense.

It was an IMS intern the previous spring who had been doing some research and came across the Ghetto Classics program in Kenya. They reached out to Elizabeth, who then got the boys to do an audition tape. (When asked why she chose those two, Elizabeth said it was because of their talent, their grades, and that, being different characters, she hoped they would bring back diverse but complementary aspects from camp that could help their fellow orchestra members.) Theresa said that comparing how the boys had been last summer—practically open-mouthed on the Hampton Jitney bus that drove them out to Long Island—and this year was an incredible change to witness.

Both Theresa and Jia felt that Kamau and Teddy had grooved

into the camp schedule and life more easily this time; the IMS kids had a jam-packed schedule that included everything from one-on-one lessons and yoga to a global exchange class where all students discussed what life was like back where they came from. "Music is a great equalizer," Theresa said. "Maybe there is a kid from Tunisia who is a more advanced player than an American kid here, and the sharing of the knowledge, it is not upward/downward, it is horizontal." Jia interrupted, saying that it wasn't just teacher to student or peer to peer, she had learned a lot from Kamau in terms of his dedication to music and the daily struggles he faced just to even get to open his cello case for practice while back home. "Last year he told me about his family and what music means to him," said Jia. "I wouldn't be able to tell you how many times I thought about him over the year. I meet people from all over the world and yet he is constantly on my mind."

She then recalled an event that had happened earlier that day in their lesson that she was still processing. At the end of the previous summer's session, Jia and two musical colleagues had given a performance of Mendelssohn's "Piano Trio No.1 in D Minor" for the campers. At the end Kamau came up to Jia and told her he wanted to play the piece she had just performed because it was one of the "most favorite things" he had ever heard.

The problem was, he did not have good access to sheet music.

So she signed the top of the page—she'd had that particular sheet music since she was in middle school—and gave it to him as a gift. "And today he brought it back to me in the lesson," she recalled with a broad smile. "The music is all dusty, there were all these specks of dirt on it. He told me he had learned the first movement. It gave me goose bumps." Jia was asked if she could even imagine the tales that piece of sheet music could tell since it had left her the year before and been carefully taken by Kamau to Nairobi and then back again to East Hampton. She shook her head vehemently from side to side. "That moment he gave it back to me, I was like, 'Wow.'"

* * *

What gave Elizabeth, Moses, Simon K., and others goose bumps was to see how the entire GC orchestra—Teddy and Kamau included—had improved over the last year, thanks in large part to the influence of one man, a young Polish composer and conductor named Jimek.

Among a certain generation of Poles, Jimek—the pseudonym of Radzimir Dębski—was a household name. Born in 1987 in Szczecin to well-known Polish composer, jazz violinist, and arranger Krzesimir Marcin Dębski and jazz singer Anna Jurksztowicz, Jimek's early years coincided with major upheavals in Polish politics and society. Unlike previous generations of Polish artists who were stuck in a limiting Communist society, by the time Jimek had come of age in a free Poland that had entered the European Union in 2004, he had not only grown up with a range of musical influences from across the globe, he also had the freedom to take advantage of studying and working abroad. By age fifteen, he had composed his first film and television scores, and at nineteen, he had co-written the soundtrack for *Ranczo*, one of the most popular shows on Polish television. Jimek went on to study composition at Warsaw's Fryderyk Chopin University of Music and then moved to Los Angeles to study at UCLA.

In 2012, Jimek's star started to shine outside of his home country when pop singer Beyoncé released her song "End of Time" on the internet and ran a contest to find the best remix version of the song. Out of over three thousand entries, Jimek's version was chosen as the winner, leading him on to other top projects including producing his first hip-hop single, "Nie Muszę Wracać," for best-selling Polish artist Pezet. In 2015, when the Polish National Radio Symphony Orchestra (NOSPR)—considered to be the best orchestra in the country—invited another popular Polish rapper, Miuosh, to perform his music with them, he invited Jimek to be the arranger. For their encore, NOSPR asked Jimek to arrange a medley of rap songs, and so he seamlessly blended songs like Jay-Z's "Girls, Girls, Girls" with Dr. Dre's "Still D.R.E." and Missy Elliott's "Get Ur Freak On" into what he called "Hip-Hop History Orchestrated." That twelve-minute piece gained him respect from music critics and rappers across the globe and has been viewed over seven million times on YouTube as of October 2022.

Elizabeth knew nothing about Jimek when his friend, Chris Szymczak, a Polish-born New Yorker who worked for UNICEF, first reached out to her via email in 2016 when he was in Nairobi for a conference and heard from a colleague about Ghetto Classics. Elizabeth, who admitted she was "crap" about checking and replying to her emails, never even saw Chris's message asking for a meeting, something that later became a joke between the two of them. But luckily Chris persevered with follow-up texts and asked if he could come out to Korogocho to hear the classically trained musicians play. Once there, Chris was blown away by what he saw and he made a video on his mobile phone and sent it to Jimek.

"In the video he said something like, 'I am in Korogocho, and it's one of the biggest slums in Nairobi, and there is this orchestra, children playing instruments, and what the hell is going on here,'" Emalka Ziabska, Jimek's producer, said. "He said, 'Jimek, you have to come here.'"

After watching the video, the lean, fetching ponytailed Polish composer agreed, telling Emalka they needed to somehow get out to Nairobi: "How and when, I do not know, but we have to go." It turned out that there were a lot of connections that Jimek and Emalka had to Kenya; they found through friends of friends a Pole who owned a travel company based in Kenya who offered his house and a translator for them, and the Polish former CEO of LOT Polish Airlines, Sebastian Mikos, was now the CEO of Kenyan Airways. Though they didn't know her at the time, Ambassador Grupinska, who all those years before had helped Elizabeth secure violins and cellos from Polish Aid, also later turned out to be a friend.

Once they were able to secure a date to go in July 2017, along with Chris and Jose Manuel Alban Juarez, a Polish-Bolivian percussionist who worked closely with Jimek and went by the moniker of Manolo, Emalka sent the hip-hop scores out to Elizabeth so the kids could familiarize themselves with the music. "She sent me a video and it was so bad, I didn't even show it to Jimek," Emalka said with a laugh, covering her face. "We knew it was going to be hard because 'Hip-Hop' is difficult to play, even for professionals. With NOSPR we had three or four rehearsals, and those guys are the best in the world." The Polish entourage brought along a cameraman with them to Nairobi as well so they could archive the rehearsals and final performance, which was eventually made into a short documentary shown on Polish television: *JIMEK + GHETTO CLASSICS*.

After the first day of rehearsal, when Jimek, dressed in a white T-shirt and jeans, had his first look around St. John's and got to know a bit more about the program, the Polish composer was devastated; the GC musicians couldn't even tune their instruments. "Tuning is something that you practice for years in musical school," he said, as the camera panned around the amphitheater and across the smoking Dandora dump. "It was the first time in my life I thought this might not work." One of the other issues was that Jimek felt the sound in the open-air amphitheater was too distracting. It wasn't just all the noise from inside the gates of St. John's, with kids playing football on the pitch, but also the lack of acoustics, which didn't allow for him to capture the sounds he needed to be picking up. After a conversation, Elizabeth asked the church if they could hold mass that week in the amphitheater so they could use the indoor chapel instead, which Jimek figured might be better for hearing the instruments mix all together. The current priest, who was from Portugal, agreed to flip-flop for the week.

For the GC musicians, the goal of those intense rehearsals (which often went on past 6:00 p.m., when St. John's gates were closed and things started to get even more dodgy around Korogocho) was an almost sold-out concert in front of over five hundred people, including everyone from Bob Collymore to top diplomats, politicians, and business executives. But for Jimek, it was about showing the kids that playing classical music could be fun. During rehearsal breaks, he got a chance to talk to a number of GC members, including Teddy and Kamau, about musical influences. It was for many of the GC members the first time a hip, cool, young musician who, of course, had the added bonus of having worked with Beyoncé, could commiserate with them over struggling to tune their instruments—Jimek was also an accomplished jazz violinist and pianist—and other general frustrations.

And he was able to explain to them that classical music was the beginning for all kinds of music, from jazz to funk, R & B, and hip-hop, tracing the roots and showing that the foundations they were learning in GC was not for naught. Their instruments, he showed them, could be made to play Tupac and 50 Cent just as easily as Beethoven and Vivaldi; that just by plucking at the violin in a different way, they could elicit sounds that were much more contemporary and experimental. "Jimek really inspired me," Teddy said. "He is so concentrated on music; he mixes classical and jazz to do his own stuff. Since I am so focused on classical, he inspired me not to concentrate on just that; there are other kinds of music I can also do."

Manolo, meanwhile, had found something of a protégé in Charity, who he worked with intensely over the week on her drumming and xylophone. "I was like, 'She is the one,'" he said. "You can feel it if you are a musician and you can watch someone playing. You can feel that she is listening to the order; she can play with the band. She is very talented for this." Manolo was so impressed with her musical potential that he hoped to help her get into music school, preferably in New York or Poland, so that she could develop even more. The percussionist felt Charity was a rare talent.

"He told me, 'I just had to play this rhythm once and she got it,'" Elizabeth said. "I asked her the other day if she wanted to be a professional percussionist and she said a big 'yes.'"

Manolo was also taken with Charity's spirit, seeing that she was a fighter. "Because she told me, 'I want to play like you but even better; I need to work like this to get out from this dump site and take my family with me,'" Manolo said. "She does not want this life." Charity's mom, Margaret, in her own quiet way, was ecstatic that Manolo not only felt her daughter was talented, but that he was willing to help her get funding for her education, and to get her out of Korogocho. "I was excited," Margaret said, adding that her daughter at home was constantly tapping things to make sound. "That is her journey, that is her life. I cannot tell her what to do. I can only teach her. And pray for her."

Jimek worked tirelessly with the GC musicians, literally going note by note in rehearsals and taking time out to explain how certain sounds, like sliding on a violin, should feel and resonate. "He had one week to create this music, and yet, because he had a brand to protect, the music had to be good enough," said Elizabeth. "So he had to find a way within himself to bring the best out of the kids. And he never complained once, and he would go home each night and change the music, spend the whole night rewriting a section because he knew it was not working. [He'd say,] 'So I will change this, so instead of playing seven notes, they only have to play three notes and the effect will still be the same.'"

Jimek also impressed upon the musicians that week that he too was still learning and though it was normal to make mistakes, it was important to keep practicing and trying to improve. By the day of the concert, Jimek was exhausted but also enthused by how far the musicians had come over those several days. It was the entire musical process, not the concert, that he felt was the most important part of the week for the Ghetto Classics musicians. The coolest moment for him was that he forgot where he was, and simply focused in on the music.

The Ghetto Classics orchestra opened the concert with a few pieces that were conducted by Kepher, who, since finishing his university degree, was moving in a few months' time to Tanzania to take up a post as musical director in a private school in Arusha. (Though his plans for Lausanne were on hold, he still dreamed of going to do a degree there in conducting.) After that set the Ghetto Classics Dancers came out and danced to a few songs, accompanied by a drummer who was a rehabilitated street child. Following intermission, Jimek came out and the audience went mad for his "Hip-Hop Orchestrated" (with additional KNYO musicians helping to fill in the gaps), cheering and clapping the most when they recognized snippets of songs like Jay-Z's "New York" and Wiz Khalifa's "Black and Yellow."

At the end of the concert for an encore, the musicians performed a piece that Jimek had composed for them, called "Beats by Ghetto Classics," which he had written on the way to the concert and that had been inspired by the sound of the colorful *matatus* (often decorated in themes, including everything from Bob Marley to Jesus and Manchester United) that drove up and down the roads.

Bob, who had told the SYO musicians when that orchestra was first founded that their job as musicians was to make people cry, shed a tear or two as he watched that day, and he later told Elizabeth that it was the best classical music concert he had ever been to.

"Jimek kind of helped to remind us of our roots," Simon K. said. "He really was a mentor."

When Jimek returned to Poland, he told the media that the concert in Nairobi had been the most important of his life, and for the members and staff of GC, it had also felt that way. For Moses, Jimek's time with the orchestra really felt like they had upped their game. "I think it was good for them to realize that instrumental music does not always have to be from the sixteenth century," Moses said. "Jimek made them understand that it is applicable today as well. A lot of high-end jazz musicians have worked with GC, but for me, Jimek was the one, and they keep talking about him."

Elizabeth agreed that the experience was something truly special for all of Ghetto Classics. "I think for both Jimek and us, we learned things about ourselves that we did not know, and our working together brought out things we did not know we had," she reflected. "We changed and it will never be the same again."

One of the guest musicians who had performed in that pivotal July concert was Anokhi Kalayil, a British flutist and university student who was interning for a month with Kevin to sort out and catalogue all the instruments kept in the container on Irene's farm. (That month, the Kenya Wildlife Service had to put up lion traps because they saw dug-up pits near the container and footprints that seemed to indicate that a leopard or cheetah may have been sleeping there, though nothing was ever caught.) She was also helping to teach at the Ruben Centre—a nonprofit community organization that included a school, a health department, a community farm, and a microfinancing project—that was located in Mukuru Kwa Ruben. The school attached to the center had been one of the original Link Up schools, and some of the more advanced students who showed promise were getting violin lessons on instruments that had been especially donated for the project. Elizabeth was impressed by how quickly they were learning and was in talks with Moses about setting up a GC orchestra at the school the next year.

One hot and windy day, as Simon K. and Anokhi were walking around Korogocho visiting schools, she got a firsthand look at the overspill from the Ngomongo dump and he gave her a briefing on what the situation was with the gangs and the corruption over getting both Dandora and Ngomongo dumps closed. He also mentioned the #stopdumpingdeathonus Twitter handle, and that got Anokhi talking to Stephen Ayoro about what more could be done to draw attention to the increasingly dire situation. "They were talking about doing a petition but they were hesitant because they did not know that much about [how] to do it," Anokhi recalled. "I was showing them that you can reach people anywhere all over the world. So they wanted to collect signatures."

Anokhi, whose parents were both born and raised in Kenya and who was about to complete her final year at the University of Warwick in the UK, found it second nature to be involved in social media and online campaigns. She offered to help them set up an online petition via avaaz.org, a US-based site that promoted activism on issues including climate change, human rights, and corruption. They spent a number of days working on wording of the petition:

> The fight against the dumping site has existed for a couple of years but the people of Korogocho have not yet received environmental integrity due to political and economic injustices. … [Our] able governor HE Mike Sonko, we kindly ask you to intervene into the matter and ensure social optimality. We have our brothers and sisters solely depending on the toxic dumping site to derive their income. We care about them and we are sure you do too. You have the capability to create a safer environment for the people of Korogocho and provide an alternative and less lethal source of income.

They were able to collect almost four hundred signatures, and though that wasn't a huge number, the campaign had activated

GC members and reinforced that there were ways and means to fight for the future of their community. Martha got involved in the campaign not only because the fire scared her but also because her mother told her that when Martha was a young girl, the area was green and farmers would graze their goats and cattle on the land.

In her lifetime, all that had changed and it sounded unbelievable to her now. "That dump puts crap in the water," she said. "I was at a church meeting and we were discussing the dump, and one person stood up and said, 'You cannot go around shouting [to] remove this thing because it is dangerous.' You have to be careful because there is big money involved and you could be killed." Regardless of the dangers, she felt it was important to be involved.

Anokhi also got to meet Salut Salon's Stephanie Schiller, who even though she had been giving Skype lessons to the GC violinists for over two years, had never until 2017 actually been to Nairobi to meet her students in person. Stephanie went with Anokhi and one of the GC drivers to the container one day and fixed five violins and two violas. Stephanie was one of those people in the GC ecosystem who thought outside the box; while giving Skype lessons was incredibly important to her, she also had other ideas that she shared with Elizabeth, including wanting to send Kevin to Hamburg, Germany, to be trained as a luthier so he would be able to fix violins and cellos. She also came up with the idea—around the same time as Elizabeth's sister Irene—that St. John's could benefit from trees. Nairobi is awash with lush, green roadside garden centers that sell trees, shrubs, and plants, yet Korogocho had barely any. She felt they could make a huge difference, especially because the illegal dump was steadily making its way to the edge of St. John's boundaries. "We were talking about what a big change it would be to have them," Stephanie said, "So the idea was born."

But the looming elections were taking precedence over everything else.

The tensions over the presidential elections that year were tied directly to the tumultuous election that had been held a decade before, where over one thousand people had died in violence between different ethnic communities. There had been extensive vote rigging in the 2007 election between Raila Odinga, a Luo, and incumbent president Mwai Kibaki, and while many election observers agreed that Odinga had won, Kibaki was sworn in again as president and violence ensued, especially in slum areas and in western Kenya. In 2013, when Odinga faced Uhuru Kenyatta (a Kikuyu), there were concerns over the electronic system that had been put in place to protect votes. There was also the issue that in incumbent strongholds there were inflated vote totals, leading observers to question Kenyatta's narrow victory. Odinga took it all the way to the Supreme Court, but Kenyatta's win was upheld and he was sworn in.

The 2017 elections were looking to be even more hotly contested, in part because since 2010, the Kenyan constitution created a decentralized system of government, where the legislative and executive arms were devolved to the forty-seven administrative counties across the country. Political parties were also known to pay people in the slums to cause disruption and violence at political events, including in places like Korogocho. Anokhi could feel the tensions each day as she went into the slum, with the gangs starting to openly carry weapons, including machetes. Elizabeth had long worried that Kenya's tribal politics could lead the country down the same horrific road that happened to its neighbor, Rwanda, in 1994, and she was particularly worried it would happen in Korogocho, which was divided along ethnic lines in certain neighborhoods. "Because remember, in Rwanda, every time it got worse," she said, "until one day, it got horrendous."

Across Nairobi, in the slum of Kibera, said to be the largest in all of East Africa, the leaders at the Shining Hope for Communities (SHOFCO) were concerned about the violence too. Kennedy Odede, a Kibera native who had witnessed the horrific 2007 violence firsthand, and his American wife, Jessica Posner, had founded the girls' school and community program. They had also co-written about their journey in *The New York Times*'s best-selling book *Find Me Unafraid: Love, Loss and Hope in an African Slum*. They also received support from Safaricom for their programming, so Jessica approached Bob because their students were about to sit for national exams and the concern was how much disruption the elections were going to cause for the girls. Safaricom ran the M-Pesa Foundation Academy, a state-of-the-art secondary school just outside of Nairobi that was aimed at highly talented but disadvantaged students, and the idea was that the girls from SHOFCO and some of the kids who lived in more vulnerable neighborhoods who were in GC could go to the camp. "Bob sent me a message, saying, 'What are we doing about your kids?'" Elizabeth said. "And I had not even thought about that."

The August 8 elections were, of course, fraught, and though observers declared the election largely free and fair, protests broke out. (A popular local expression went that whoever captures the presidency is the one whose "turn it is to eat" for the next five years, as the rest are left out in the cold.[5] While Kenya had over forty ethnic groups, up to that point three of the country's four presidents since independence had been Kikuyu. William Ruto, elected in August 2022, is from the Kalenjin ethnic group.) Odinga and his supporters took the case to the country's Supreme Court. Within GC, there weren't a lot of ethnic issues, in part, Simon K. believed, because those who had come of age in the 1990s and witnessed what happened had become neighbors and friends. They were, for the most part, able to coexist peacefully. "They have grown up together here, so they do not really attack each other when there are problems," Simon K. said. "But people are moving in from the villages and they do not know each other."

And although a GC tutor's mother, who was Luo, sent some nasty messages to Elizabeth and Simon K. (both Kikuyu), there wasn't much else that infiltrated GC during the elections. (The tutor's mother later apologized, and her son was mortified by the whole interaction.) However, some neighborhoods like Lucky Summer, which were more mixed, and were where Teddy and Charity lived, saw much violence. "During the elections, we were just wrapped up indoors for three days," Margaret, Charity's mother, said. "Those

---

5 Gadjanova, Elena, "Kenya's 2017 Election and its Aftermath" (Max Planck Institute for the Study of Religious and Ethnic Diversity, Göttingen, February 20, 2019).

who are making violence and those who are funding it, they are just idle people who want to steal things. They are not bad people as such but when they start breaking things, that's when you get annoyed, you react, and there is violence."

Teddy and Kamau, of course, were safely tucked thousands of miles away in East Hampton while a number of their GC colleagues were sent for two weeks to the M-Pesa camp. "The camp was a real positive," said Hecky Odera, SHOFCO's director of education. "I think it was beneficial for our girls and for the GC children. It was a safe place to be. We do not have a music club, so that seed was planted by GC; that interaction and exchange was a big plus." There was also talk that once everything calmed down, GC might look at helping set up a music program for the SHOFCO girls.

The Supreme Court ruled in September 2017 that the election results were null and void and that another election should take place in October, which Odinga boycotted, claiming it would not be fair. President Kenyatta was declared the victor, again, with ninety-eight percent of the vote and though skirmishes broke out, the real unrest for Korogocho came almost a month later. The Supreme Court was asked to rule again in the elections, this time on the legality of the October rerun election. The vote had been widely boycotted by the opposition and denounced by Odinga as a sham; he left the country on a ten-day speaking tour in Europe and the US after withdrawing from the election. Upon his return, violence erupted again and SHOFCO and GC asked Safaricom to set up another camp.

Kids who were seen as vulnerable, including Teddy and Kamau, who had been back from the US for a few months, were told to arrive at the Thika Road Mall (TRM) at a specified time because it was too dangerous to get the kids rounded up at St. John's. "All these GC members kept arriving at the mall, running in, you could hear gunshots and it felt shocking and scary," Kamau remembered. The cellist said it felt like they were in a movie, and they watched as, one by one, GC members would run into the mall, safe. "You know, we were just glad they had made it."

On one side of Korogocho there were almost no problems, but at St. John's—coming from the Kariobangi side—gangs created a border so that no one could pass through without paying money or being beaten. Charity's mother escorted her through Lucky Summer to get her to Erick's house, which had been a meeting place for a number of the kids. "We went through a mixed area and there was police and tear gas," Charity recalled. "It got really bad and we had to hide at one point because we saw some people bearing down on a man, shouting, 'Kill him, kill him!'"

Elizabeth was particularly worried about Simon M., who got caught up in the midst of the rioting and violence. He and his mother lived in a predominantly Kikuyu neighborhood, but it was a border area with a Luo one. "It was anarchy," Elizabeth said. "Simon M. called, desperate for help as his house was surrounded by hostile people getting ready to attack his family." Elizabeth begged him to come to the meeting point at TRM, but Simon M. refused to leave his mother, Margaret.

"It was one of the worst experiences I have ever had," Simon M. remembered stoically. "For four days, it was crazy like hell." The sensitive trombonist was scared and called Elizabeth a number of times over the next few days, crying and explaining the situation as she heard gunshots and screaming in the background.

She promised Simon M. she would do whatever it took to get him out, even—unrealistically—send a helicopter in to rescue him. Elizabeth even sent Simon K. in to try and get them, but he could not get through the makeshift checkpoints that had been set up. Simon M., his mother Margaret, and around one hundred women and children were forced to live outside, taking shelter within the dump site. "We were with my mother the whole time, protecting her," Simon M. said. "I kept asking her to 'move, move, move' to the other side of the dump. I know my responsibilities are to take care of her." They dodged broken glass and locally made *mishale* (arrows) being thrown at them. "Even boys my age were fighting," he said. "I could not risk going to fight." Simon M. and his mom eventually got police protection but because she had not been able to work for several days, they were short on money, had no food, and their home had been damaged during the riots. Though Elizabeth had physically not been able to go in and save him, Ghetto Classics was able to give him funds and food, which was a proverbial lifeline.

For those who were able to make it to the M-Pesa camp, it was a welcome respite from the violence they had witnessed over the last several months. "We would wake up early in the morning, play music, take a break, and play music again," Kamau said, almost as if he was describing his East Hampton camp experience. "So you find we keep improving our music ability." When asked what ethnic group his family was from, Kamau paused and then said with a cautious laugh and a smile, "I am Kenyan."

Ten

While Simon M., Charity, Teddy, Kamau, and the rest of her GC friends and colleagues were mingling and messing around during intermission, enjoying the free soda and juice being served at the plush, newly opened Trademark Hotel, Celine gave a tight-lipped smile and looked like she might be about to be sick. Jorge had come back to Nairobi for a May 2018 fundraising concert for KNYO—ten years to the month that GC was founded—and she had been chosen to play the well-known opening clarinet riff of George Gershwin's "Rhapsody in Blue." She had been practicing for weeks and while she knew it backwards and forwards, she couldn't help but feel nervous and wound up. Dressed like the rest of the orchestra, in a black top and black trousers, she stood back from the rest of them, making pained small talk with audience members, her mind obviously elsewhere.

But once she was back on the stage in the big beige ballroom and was given the cue by the song's guest conductor, Bill Rowe, Celine began her solo, strong and confident. All her worry and stress had been for naught, as she nailed the music, not a squeaking reed vibration or note out of place. There were random scattered claps for her as she finished, for which she beamed and instantly relaxed. Soon Jorge, in an elegantly cut black suit with no tie and a neat five o'clock shadow, took over the piece, dazzling the well-heeled audience with his powerful yet light rendition of the famous jazz-infused 1924 composition. Jorge and Elizabeth then both spoke to the two hundred or so assembled guests, many of whom had been supporters of the Art of Music Foundation for years.

While Jorge discussed the power of music in terms of both helping him process his father's death when he was a teen and in his work with his musical foundation in Mexico, Elizabeth spoke about KNYO and particularly focused on the fact that a number of GC members were also part of the orchestra. She then told the story of Kepher running through the freshly cut grass at the US Embassy all those years ago, and how in six years he had gone from the depressed teen relegated to sleeping amid the church pews to conducting for Pope Francis and President Kenyatta, arranging and composing music, and his current position as a music teacher in Tanzania. It was a musical Cinderella story and the crowd ate it up.

Levi then took up the baton and ended the concert with works that included "Mars" by Gustav Holst, "Finlandia" by Jean Sibelius, and Kepher's orchestral adaptation of "Malaika." They also did a rousing strings version of "Amavolovolo," a beautiful South African folk song that put a tingle down the spine, with musicians walking amongst the audience as they played. It was one of those special moments that only music can seem to evoke—it had that power to unite people by touching something primeval in everyone at the same time. In those precious few moments, it felt like everything was right with the universe and it was all going to be okay.

On one hand, the story of Kepher drilled home just how much Ghetto Classics had accomplished over the decade, not only in terms of teaching thousands of young people music but also helping change the trajectory of many for the better. Likely this would be something that would help get donors to find just a bit more money in their pocketbooks. But it also slightly smacked of what Levi had warned the GC musicians about a few years before: while their backstory was a powerful one, there would eventually have to come a time that it was just that, an intriguing side note versus something that defined them as an orchestra. While over the years they had musically been given preferential treatment because of where they had come from, the burden was on them now to prove that they were also worthy musicians in their own right. While Kepher wasn't in the audience that evening to hear Elizabeth regale his story, he'd heard a similar version of it many times before, and he—along with a number of GC members who also confided this fact—was sick of it.

* * *

A few nights before the KNYO concert, Elizabeth, Levi,

and Jorge sat down under the sticky night sky just as fat droplets of rain started slamming down on the deck patio of an outdoor café at Nairobi's Village Market. As waiters feverishly ran over to put up a large umbrella to protect them from the downpour, the three started talking about their concerns for Kepher. For years GC had been the love of Kepher's life. "For me, Ghetto Classics is my number one," he had said just a year before. "I would rather drop other orchestras and go Ghetto Classics. Those people, I owe them. It is because of them that I got to this level. [I] am always honored and I don't take it for granted." Yet since then, he'd developed cynical feelings towards Elizabeth, Levi, and the orchestra.

When he was back in Nairobi over the Easter holidays, Kepher hadn't come around to visit, something that had hurt a number of GC members as well as Elizabeth. For a close-knit group, especially those who had been through so much together over the years, it felt like he had disowned them. Jorge had invited Kepher to come to Lausanne for three months to work on his conducting in autumn 2018 and while the invitation was still open, Jorge was admittedly perplexed by his behavior towards GC and Elizabeth.

The three were concerned whether Kepher was being treated fairly at the international school where he was teaching—he had implied there had been some problems—but they were also confused and troubled by his apparent 180-degree turn against GC. They all speculated that maybe he was believing his own press, having been written about in local papers when he'd recently travelled to South Korea and North Carolina, and his pride was starting to get the better of him. To Levi and Elizabeth, it felt as if he wanted to erase his history with GC.

However, Kepher wasn't the only one who was feeling growing pains within GC. A number of the older members, including Emily, Martha, and Simon K. had started questioning their role within the orchestra and the overall organization.

For Martha and Emily, they loved their time in GC, but music was not their burning passion. Emily was doing a diploma in journalism and she was also running a media-training course in Korogocho for a Swedish NGO. Plus she also practiced taekwondo weekly. Meanwhile, Martha had started a certificate course in filmmaking and since her mother had gone "up country" for several months to build a new house, she was more focused on getting money for survival. "Music gets jealous; it requires a lot of time," Martha said, explaining that she didn't think she was improving much anymore because her priorities were elsewhere. The two women were good friends, having bonded over the years. They not only had fun together in the violin section, they'd also shared a few harrowing times, including during the riots in November 2017. As skirmishes erupted and gunshots were fired, they ran through the streets of Korogocho, finally finding refuge in Emily's studio flat, where they hid out for three hours as they thought the world was caving in.

For some time now they both had become critical of how GC was run, feeling that over the years some people within the program, like Precious and Celine, had been given preferential treatment over others. But they also felt that as young adults, they didn't have much of a say in what happened within GC anymore. While the primary and secondary school kids had their own GC leadership council (overseen by Simon K.) there was nothing to represent them and their ideas. And since Martha and Emily weren't planning to pursue music as a career and didn't do much tutoring, they felt left out of the loop, and that those who wanted a career in music got more opportunities, which made sense, but the young women didn't see it that way. Their age also was a problem in that they were no longer minors, and that had created some conflicts.

In February 2018, at the Safaricom Jazz Festival, GC had performed a selection of jazz music with Jimek—that year again in the unfortunate early slot—and afterwards Martha and some of the tutors, who were all over eighteen, started drinking. (The legal drinking age in Kenya is eighteen.) Someone from Safaricom noticed after a time that the group was getting rowdy and they were worried because there were underage GC kids with them. Elizabeth found Martha and another young woman, Irene, and reprimanded them for having alcohol. Martha at first straight-up lied to her, saying she was drinking Coke when Elizabeth knew it was Guinness. "I had to lecture them about how to behave when they are mentors and tutors," Elizabeth said. "That was not the place or time to get drunk. Martha apologized, while Irene just glared." They put their drinks down and went to watch the music with the rest of the kids. Elizabeth, meanwhile, was horrified at the thought of them going home to their parents drunk from a GC event.

Neither Emily nor Martha was quite sure how to leave GC, and Elizabeth wasn't quite sure either. "I keep trying to see how I can graduate [the older ones] but they are family, so I cannot kick them out," Elizabeth said. "Right now, my problem is with my twenty-somethings. It's independence issues, I guess. It's a new frontier I need to figure out." There wasn't any kind of alumni network set up, and if they were no longer a part of the orchestra, it would not only mean that the women wouldn't see their friends on a weekly basis, but they would lose all the advantages they had gotten used to over the years.

For example, Emily, always the networker, had the access to meet with Jorge when he was in town for the KNYO concert. She discussed with him the possibility that when the new music center that he was trying to raise money for was built and opened, it could also serve as something of an arts center. She pitched him the idea of doing an exhibition on gender-based violence in the slums using photographs taken by the women themselves. Jorge was taken with the idea, not only because it could be an important way for women and girls to chronicle their lives and experiences, but also because Emily had a great ability to broaden the remit of her GC experience.

Both women, like Kepher, were also tired of GC being presented, as they saw it, as some kind of sob story. The orchestra's name alone implied their background, so they weren't just seen as any youth orchestra but one where they felt that audiences almost gawped in amazement at their accomplishments. "Why can't we just be an orchestra?" Emily asked rhetorically over dinner one evening. "Yes, we have come from hard lives in Korogocho, but constantly being used for our slum roots now feels insincere somehow." Yet Emily,

Martha, and Kepher seemed to miss a great irony: they happily reaped the advantages of being in a slum orchestra when it suited them, but they also hated that they were treated and defined in a special way because of where they were from.

It was a subject that Jorge and Kepher spoke at length about throughout 2018. Kepher told his mentor that he felt used by GC, a ghetto poster boy whose backstory raised money for the organization. "I explained to him that he was not being used, that GC needed an example and that [for] us as foundations, we need to show results, and he was a result, a very beautiful result of a very beautiful program," Jorge said. "Ghetto Classics needed an image, and that is why he was being—in quotes—used. I told him that I also need [illustrations] of people whose lives we have changed in Mexico." Organizations, he explained, needed examples to raise more money that would in turn would help more young people. And without money, there was no Ghetto Classics.

After a decade, Simon K. had also reached a crossroads with GC. He loved the organization, no doubt. But many things had started to wear him down. One reason was the basic fact that being at St. John's every day was not great for his health. Both he and Peter sometimes were forced to go home early because the sulfur-smelling smoke wafting into their office was so bad it made their eyes red. (Simon K. no longer lived in Korogocho.) Other support staff members had recently moved to a new office—they had never worked at St. John's but had been in a few different locales around Nairobi over the years—and Simon K. wanted to work from there, in part because he felt that not being physically in the main office meant he was often left out of a lot of big decisions. "I have the title of manager," he said over pizza at the Garden City Mall. "But I don't have the role in the overall big picture. If I was truly the manager, I would also be involved more financially [and] make [more] management decisions."

Simon K. also pointed to the fact that in July 2018, fifteen of the GC members had been invited to go to Wroclaw, Poland, to perform at the Brave Festival with Jimek, which was a thrill because it would be GC's international debut. Celine, Kamau, Charity, Simon M., and Teddy were among those Simon K. had picked to go, and he had also included himself on the list. "I shared the names of the kids but Elizabeth cancelled my name on the form," Simon K. said, adding that he had a passport from when he travelled to Scotland a few years before. "I am not going. Why is my name not on the list when I am the manager? So there is a disconnect."

Meanwhile within St. John's, there seemed to be a constant battle between the parish, the school, and GC. While some priests had supported their work over the years, others had not. One of the most recent Catholic fathers had wanted to charge GC rent, which Elizabeth said she was willing to pay. But it was something that Simon K. put his foot down over, not only out of principle, but also the fact that St. John's benefited a lot from Ghetto Classics being there. It was a similar battle Simon K. had fought years earlier with the priest who replaced Father John. "The politics never ends," he said with a deep sigh.

The wider Korogocho community also was tiring him. Simon had long been frustrated that GC was something of a walk-in center on weekends—Orchestras B and C practiced on Saturdays, while Orchestra A continued to run on Sundays—and he wanted to only do intakes twice a year because he felt it was disruptive to the teaching to constantly have new students coming in. But Elizabeth had long ago put the kibosh on that, saying that if they waited to help a child who came in looking for some interaction and attention, that child could be forever lost. It frustrated him to constantly have new people joining, and it was something he couldn't sometimes keep track of. He also had to keep the gang members happy, but at arms' length so they would not cause trouble for GC, such as when visitors and dignitaries came to visit. Within Korogocho, many parents understood that GC was a social program that was helping kids, yet others had expectations and didn't understand, for example, why some children had their school fees paid for while others did not. It was need-based, Simon K. would explain to them. But in a place like Korogocho, they would argue, everyone was needy.

He also felt he was stagnant and needed a challenge. Elizabeth had realized this and charged him with running the new GC Mukuru Kwa Ruben program that had begun in April 2018. But with the head of that program, Joseph Muhindi, a seemingly competent Link Up teacher and manager, even that wasn't inspiring him. If Simon K. could get the financing, he hoped to do a master's degree in development. It was a subject close to his heart, not only because he'd grown up and seen firsthand how development programs did and did not work, but also having worked for GC for so many years, he wanted to have the academic qualifications to better understand how to run an efficient and sustainable program. He'd done his undergraduate degree in music at the Technical University of Kenya. (In doing his dissertation on the impact of GC as a social program, his professor pointed out that there were no statistics to back up the impact that he was writing about, which equally intrigued and frustrated him.) While Ghetto Classics was part of his DNA, it was time to move on.

Simon K. applied for and was accepted at School of Oriental and African Studies (SOAS) University of London for their music in development graduate program (he was also accepted to a general music education MA at the University of Georgia in the US). While he was excited by the prospect, not only to improve his education, but also to have some time away from Kenya, he also had thought a lot about what his leaving would mean for GC and who could take over his role. It would not be easy to fill his shoes, but he felt that his job could be split between Peter and Alex Kimathi, a friend of Simon K.'s from the university who had been the GC office administrator at St. John's since 2015. Though shy, Peter was good with community outreach and his background in social work was certainly an added benefit for the job. Alex, meanwhile, could run the day-to-day operations. Kevin could assist both of them.

Kevin's strengths were that he was very good at follow-up and seeing things through, while Simon K. was very good with the community relations. "Simon K. does not like to annoy anyone. He is a diplomat; he wants to be friends with everyone," Elizabeth said. "Kevin does not give a toss, which is not good either, but they complement each other." But the men seriously butted heads. One of the things they had clashed on over the years was that Simon K. felt that any time they went out into the community they represented Ghetto Classics, and with neither of them living in the slum anymore, he felt they needed to carry themselves in a certain way while out in the community to maintain a positive image. So, he was livid one day when they were driving through Korogocho, and Kevin, dressed in a Ghetto Classics T-shirt, reportedly jumped out of the car to shake hands and talk with some known drug dealers who they had just seen making a sale. He fought with Kevin, telling him it looked bad for the organization—in GC gear no less—to be seen warmly greeting criminals.

Kevin himself had been having a bad run of it lately anyway; earlier in the year he'd been found with a stolen mobile phone, which it turned out had been the property of someone who had been murdered. (In Kenya when you buy an expensive mobile telephone, you have to register the phone and there is a tracking device.) The police had come looking for him and had arrested him at St. John's in front of a number of the kids. Kevin spent a few nights in jail. He swore to Elizabeth, who let him sweat it out before she bailed him out because she wanted him to understand the seriousness of the incident, that a friend had given him the phone and he knew nothing about its tragic and troubled history. Meanwhile, Simon K. buttered up a few of the local police to not only get the bail money reduced but also to make sure Kevin would not be "tagged," where police keep their eyes on certain people in the slum who they might later target if they were investigating crimes. (Simon K.'s eldest brother, who had been in a gang, had been tagged. He was later shot and killed by police. So Simon K. knew the dangers if someone was deemed to be trouble.) There had also been an incident when the soprano saxophone of one of GC's players went missing for about a month from the music room/office at St. John's.

Everyone blamed Kevin. Elizabeth got a friend who was high up in the Criminal Investigation Department to question him, along with Simon K., Alex, and a few others about the missing instrument. The young men were terrified, saying that whoever took it had probably just meant to borrow it for a gig and for some reason was late in returning it. Soon after, the soprano saxophone miraculously turned up in a spare room near the toilets in the St. John's community building, and the truth about what happened remained a mystery. Elizabeth was concerned not only about the lying, but that everyone pointed a finger at Kevin, who she felt was either not telling the truth or there was a conspiracy against him. For Kevin, the whole thing had been a bad experience that revealed some deep tensions between himself and some of the GC staff.

He felt it was partially to do with the fact that since the Art of Music Foundation had hired him on in September 2017, he had authority over some things within GC and that had created some jealousies. "I am not on good terms with some of them," he said in May 2018. "I try to tell them the truth and then they feel like, 'You used to be our friend and we would do things with you.'" The flare-ups subsided and things soon ironed themselves out. Kevin, rightly shaken by those few incidents, put his head down and avoided trouble. He was desperate to get to Germany to train to be a luthier, but his mother, afraid of yet another child leaving her, had hidden his birth certificate, making it impossible to get a passport.

* * *

Beyond the ragged and rusty chain-linked fence behind the community center lay a fifteen-meter-wide and fifteen-meter-long section of land that was flat before a drop-off into the Ngomongo dump. Over time the natural border had become overgrown with bushes and garbage. And lots of snakes. "We kill them," Kevin said with a slight grin as he walked away from the edge of the fence during a guided tour of St. John's in mid-2018. Stephanie, from Salut Salon, and Irene, Elizabeth's sister, had an idea to create a bit of green space there. It would serve not only as a demarcation border, but also a beautification project that the GC kids could take pride in and tend to. In 2018 it was finally coming to fruition. GC got tires from the gang in the dump, which the members painted white, and GC also bought broken glass from the gang and put it in the dirt for some sparkle.

During the cleanup, which took about a week in early April, dozens of GC kids, staff, some children from the community, and even a few members of the local gang who ran the Ngomongo dump, got to work removing the rubbish, plastic, and bamboo, and then planting seedlings of grass. "We had the gangs get involved because you can never do something independently here," Kevin said. "You have to involve them so they feel they are a part of this, to understand what we are doing and not cause us problems." On the day of the official opening of the garden, various people, including dignitaries, local leaders, and gang members planted sixty trees and shrubs along the edge of the natural border. As they planted, Stephanie, along with the strings, played music. "She said plants need music to grow," Elizabeth recalled with a chuckle. The then-British high commissioner, Nic Hailey, came in his personal capacity, planted a tree, and joined the strings on his violin. Stephanie planted a pomegranate tree for Salut Salon, donated by Elizabeth's brother, Allan, who unexpectedly passed away later that year.

In the same month that St. John's was getting its green on, GC Mukuru Kwa Ruben, the first orchestra they were running outside of Korogocho, was officially launched at the Ruben Centre. The expansion of the GC orchestra that Bob had long wanted was now happening and it was an important new step for the Art of Music Foundation.

Lewinsky Atieno, a teacher at GC Mukuru Kwa Ruben, got her first name from the infamous 1998 sex scandal that almost brought down President Bill Clinton. While all of the US was enthralled in the details of the president's lurid affair with intern Monica Lewinsky, the future GC clarinetist's mom, who was pregnant with her at the time, was enthralled with the name. "I guess my mom really liked it," laughed Lewinsky, an exceedingly pretty young woman with blindingly white straight teeth and a smile that took up her entire face. Lewinsky, who was one of Celine's pupils and also a member of KNYO, had been teaching since the Mukuru Kwa Ruben orchestra program had started, and so far, she loved it. "It's fun because I am doing what I like," she said, adding that having finished form four the year before, she eventually wanted to do a business degree. "I try to teach a little at GC when Celine is not around," she said, drinking chai tea and eating a fried doughnut in the hot Saturday sun at the Ruben Centre in May 2018. "I have been working on my shyness, so this is helping," she said with a smile. Though there was not yet a close bond between the teachers and students, Lewinsky said she felt there were some kids who were talented and were very attentive in lessons.

As one of the original Link Up schools from 2016, the center, which was originally founded as a school in 1986 by the Catholic Christian Brothers African Province, had a strong infrastructure in place within the slum. The background of Mukuru Kwa Ruben was different from Korogocho, with its population of over six hundred thousand. It was larger and had an industrial feel because it was built near the railway line with large concrete boulders scattered everywhere along the bumpy roads—but many of the problems of poverty, crime, abuse, and drugs were the same. For Elizabeth and Moses, having a willing and eager partner was an essential reason why they decided to expand the orchestra program there. "We figured it would be the fastest way to grow it, to move to another place," said Moses. "The infrastructure was there, the support from the school administration was there, and the accessibility for safety was another reason why we selected that. We thought we could fly much faster and have an orchestra quicker at Mukuru."

Plus, the students had shown a real willingness to advance beyond the Link Up program, thanks to Joseph, who had been their original Link Up teacher and was now running the Saturday morning orchestra program with an initial cohort of forty-eight kids. "It is really exciting from my point of view to be the first GC program outside of Korogocho," said Joseph, a piano and flute player who was a graduate of the Nairobi School. "To see my kids who I taught on the recorder now playing trombone, it is quite rewarding."

David Otieno, one of GC's most proficient violin tutors who was also earmarked to go to Poland, was in an outdoor stairwell working with four aspiring violinists while other students were in various classrooms practicing scales and "Twinkle, Twinkle, Little Star." Eight budding musicians were in one room being introduced to the cellos, the first day they had them at the school. The teacher asked if anyone wanted to come up and pluck a note. One girl, in a turquoise headscarf, pink-and-white skirt, and flip-flops, bravely jumped out of her seat, had a go, and then gave her teacher a high five before sitting back down.

Joseph, smartly dressed in a white shirt, jeans, and black shoes, said that he was personally interested to find out if music was helping the kids do better in school. "I was checking in their end of term exams and you see they are improving," he said, standing outside one of the classrooms where the kids were rehearsing. "The history and Swahili teachers say that the kids in the music program are doing really well. One boy improved a lot in class, and we suspect it is because of the music. He is very active and always the first person to arrive. We see courage, confidence, and empowerment."

Joseph also felt that, depending on the success of GC Mukuru Kwa Ruben, there would be opportunities to expand to Mombasa, as well as to Kisumu and Naivasha. "And then it could move across the country," he said. "That would be so amazing. I feel at the moment things are moving and growing. We plan to play in churches; we want to spread music into the community." Joseph also credited Elizabeth for being a harbinger for change for classical music in the country as a whole. "I think she created a blueprint for music in Kenya," he said. "There is something a musician once told me: 'If you want to have an audience, you have to create an audience.' So that is what she has done; she has filled a big vacuum."

That was something that Eric Booth had long felt about the GC program overall. Having visited over two dozen global Sistema projects and having written an entire book (along with music writer Tricia Tunstall) on the subject of Sistema programs, he felt that what made GC unique in the world—alongside the Philippines's Ang Misyon program and El Sistema in Venezuela—was that Elizabeth had helped create a musical ladder for kids to climb. That musicians could move onwards and upwards in their playing and skills didn't just end when they left GC. "In Nairobi, with the different levels of accomplishment and the chance to move up to KNYO, SYO, and the Nairobi Orchestra, there is an organic way to achieve an advanced level," he said. And GC members did not have to put their instruments away once they had graduated from secondary school; music was something they could pursue as a hobby and passion for a lifetime.

Eleven

Every summer since 2005 in the charming western Polish city of Wroclaw, which before World War II had been the charming eastern German city of Breslau, the Brave Festival has brought musicians from across the globe to showcase their musical and cultural traditions during a weeklong festival. A month after Jimek, Manolo, and Emalka had been in Nairobi for the jazz festival in 2018, the program director for the festival reached out to Elizabeth to see about bringing members of GC over to play at Brave, mentioning that he had read about the orchestra online. She passed along Emalka's contacts to him, and he was at first confused, not knowing there was any connection between GC, Poland, and one of the country's biggest musical composers. "It was crazy," Emalka said about the randomness of it all. "We never thought to take them from Kenya to Poland." They connected and tried to figure out how to get Ghetto Classics to Wroclaw.

After Simon K. came up with the list of fifteen or so musicians who would be mature enough and good enough to go, Elizabeth got moving on getting birth certificates and passports for those who needed them, and visas for everyone. It was a lot of work, with Elizabeth not only using up favors from various contacts within the Kenyan government, but also reaching out to Ambassador Grupinska, who was now living back in Warsaw. "She pushed the Polish Embassy," said Emalka. "[This was] maybe not all the things that needed to be done, but it was in part from her."

Wamocho was one of the people on the list because he would be conducting the orchestra in both a stand-alone afternoon performance and as part of the evening concert that would feature Jimek. One of the works they wanted to play was Kepher's orchestral arrangement of "Malaika," which he named "Malaika Variations," that the KNYO had performed in May. Kepher got wind that Wamocho wanted to perform the piece in Wroclaw and he was livid. He sent a WhatsApp to Wamocho saying that he was angered that no one had asked his consent, and feeling it was a breach of copyright. Kepher also asked that GC not perform the arrangement again.

Technically, of course, he was right, but Elizabeth and Wamocho were floored that in a Shakespearean turn, he had given them a cease and desist for using his music. It was biting off the proverbial hand that had in the past literally and figuratively fed him. It was also shortsighted on Kepher's part because the arrangement would have been that much richer in its provenance to be performed internationally at a well-beloved festival in Europe.

While all this was happening in the background, Elizabeth was not only scrambling to get the Ministry of Education clearance for the GC kids for the Poland trip, but she was also exchanging emails and texts with Auma Obama, the half-sister of the former US president who was coming to Kenya in July to open a leisure center in the Obama family's ancestral village in western Kenya. Auma, a sociologist and community activist, was a friend of one of Elizabeth's sisters-in-law and also was an acquaintance of Stephanie, who, when she was in town in April for the tree planting, organized a meeting between herself, Auma, and Elizabeth. Auma later invited Elizabeth and GC to the center's opening on July 18, where seventeen members, including Simon K., would perform "Daima Kenya," while its composer Eric Wainaina, a popular Kenyan singer-songwriter, would sing.

Elizabeth was excited but disappointed because she would already be in Poland with the GC kids, but she told Auma that of course GC would love to be involved. But she soon after got another message, this time from a big Kenyan PR company that handled press for President Obama, whose father had been a senior Kenyan government economist and was a central figure in President Obama's 1995 memoir, *Dreams from My Father*. They asked if a small number of GC members would be interested to come play at an intimate dinner that President Obama would be hosting at the Kempinski Hotel in Nairobi on July 15. She said an ecstatic "YES!" and then realized it was the same evening as their flight to Poland. Elizabeth pondered how she could see her musicians play for Barack Obama while also somehow catching her flight. It was a timing gamble, but one she was ready to take.

When deciding which members she would bring to the five-star hotel to perform, she specifically chose three of them—Simon M., flutist Elvis Otieno, and percussionist Johnson Osio—because their Polish visas had not yet come through and it looked like they wouldn't be able to go to Poland. Elizabeth kept a lid on telling the musicians (there were six of them in the end) who they would be performing for until just a few days before the concert. She also invited Avery Waite, a Juilliard-trained American cellist and the executive director of MusAid—a nonprofit specializing in global music education—who was visiting with GC for three weeks, to also perform with them. The day before the concert, she did a dry run, going to the hotel to meet with the Secret Service, and she was given strict orders by the PR firm to not make any attempts to speak with the president. As soon as they were done playing, they were to immediately leave, which worked well for her travel plans but seemed a bit of a bummer that they wouldn't meet President Obama.

The next day Elizabeth was rightly stressed out; the GC group of musicians going to Poland, sans Simon M., Elvis, and Osio (his nickname), were headed to the airport but they had to wait to check in until Elizabeth got there. Meanwhile, though Avery and the teens had planned to do a run-through of the two songs they were going to perform—a Kenyan folk song called "Todii," and "Mai Nozipo," which was written by Zimbabwe's Dumisani Maraire and the Kronos Quartet—but things at St. John's were too hectic because of all the last minute prep for the musicians going to Poland and those practicing for the other Obama performance in a few days' time. So, Avery and the musicians headed over directly to the Kempinski in the GC van.

Upon arrival they were told that they could not come through the front entrance of the hotel. Elizabeth, who arrived separately and was told she could go through the front lobby, was furious that her kids were made to go through the service entrance, where they had to wait outside for almost two hours. In the end though, it turned out to be a productive time because the musicians got to practice (though hotel staff came out to ask them to stop playing because they were making too much noise) and Elizabeth had a chance to take in how the musicians looked and what they brought with them. And she was dumbfounded.

Two of the girls, Tracy and trumpeter Betty Mwende, had worn sandals, and the musicians had also brought beaten-up old wooden music stands. "I was like, 'We are playing for President Obama! Where are the decent looking stands?'" she recalled. "I sent a message to Irene, Levi, and Duncan with pictures of the shoes and music stands and asked them, 'So do we stay authentic or do we look good?'" In the end, she decided she wanted them to look properly presentable, so she sent Mark, one of the GC drivers, to the container to get better looking stands, and to a nearby mall to get the girls decent shoes.

Finally, they were brought inside to the small room where the dinner was to be held and the guests were all assembled, excluding President Obama. "I was struck by how intimate the event was," said Avery. "I had seen Obama a few times before, but it was in the context of these massive political rallies and this was a very small space, twenty people and us." Though the kids were likely nervous, they didn't show it. "They were all really composed because I think they perform so much that they are ready to go under any situation," Avery said. "It is not that they have complete training on their instruments by any means but in terms of being natural performers, they have got that down." President Obama, who had been meeting with President Kenyatta, finally came in without any pomp and circumstance. "We weren't told he was coming and then all of a sudden he was there," Tracy recalled. "I thought he would be taller but he was average height, which surprised me a little."

After being introduced to the musicians, Elizabeth gave a short speech about GC and how they were learning classical music. She then gave a specific hat tip to Michael Joseph, one of the evening's guests, for having been so supportive in the early years to the Art of Music activities. The president turned to Michael, thanking him for supporting the projects, and then congratulated Elizabeth on the work that she and the orchestra had done over the years. After first performing "Todii," President Obama jovially told them, "When I take Michelle to the opera, I would not hear *that* music. You guys know how to groove." Elizabeth laughed and told him that this was African classical music. Avery and the kids also nervously chuckled and got ready for the next song. "I think he thought we were going to play Mozart or something," Avery said, "but he was tickled." Once they finished, he asked them if they wanted a photo—they all answered, "Yes, PLEASE"—and he made a bit more small talk with them. "Let me tell you, he knows how to make you love him," said Elizabeth. "He was just so charming [and] it was natural." He didn't, however, attempt any Swahili.

Afterwards, Elizabeth sped off to the airport and Avery went with the kids to a local mall to get some dinner. They were all talking animatedly, excited that it had gone well, and the moment finally starting to sink in. Avery told them that what struck him was that if a similar situation were to happen in the US, an orchestra would have spent months getting ready for the performance, with everything just perfect. There was something refreshing in how organic and relaxed it all had been that evening. "It was not an overwrought, incredibly stressful thing that I kind of expected, given my context," Avery said. When he told them that this was an amazing experience that they could tell everyone about for the rest of their lives, they all kind of laughed. "They told me, 'It does not matter if we tell everyone because no one will believe us anyway,'" he said. "I think legitimately it was a private thing for them. But for me, it was pretty amazing what they had just [done], knowing their background and where they were going back to that night."

Tracy, a sweet young woman who had grown up with a convict father who had been violent with the family, said that it was one of the high points of her life. She added that though she did tell people, their reaction was exactly how the GC members that night had suspected it would be. "People said to me, 'You have been watching too many movies,' and did not believe me when I told people in Korogocho the next day," she said with a giggle. A few months later, GC received a photo of the event, with President Obama facing the camera, which Tracy jokingly referred to as "the butt photo" because several of them had their backs to the camera and their faces were obscured. That picture hangs in the GC offices at St. John's.

Meanwhile, the Polish-bound GC musicians landed the next day in a rainy Warsaw and then took a bus to Wroclaw. It was a long, tiring trip but the kids—and Elizabeth—were excited. Despite the weather, wrapped up in sweatshirts, hats, and using *shuka* shawls to keep the summer drizzle off their heads, the musicians had a few days for sightseeing. Kamau found a larger-than-life contemporary statue of a cello that he cheekily posed next to while the whole group got a photo with a street art installation of gnomes playing in an orchestra. (Small gnome statues are scattered across Wroclaw in a nod to the Orange Alternative, which was an anti-Soviet resistance movement that helped bring down the country's Communist regime in the 1980s.) They also tried new cuisine while exploring the city. "The food was totally weird," recalled Wamocho. "There was a time they brought some liver in some salad. No one among us could eat it. Everything had a sour taste, but we started getting used to it." Charity agreed, adding that the only food they loved was breakfast. "We are used to having *ugali* (a cornmeal porridge) at every meal," she said, cackling from the memory. "We always eat it, so we were weak, we were dying."

Luckily, Elizabeth's magic wand still worked even when she wasn't in Kenya, with Simon M.'s, Elvis's, and Osio's visas coming through on Monday, the same day that the other GC members headed out to perform at the opening of the Auma Obama's Sauti Kuu Foundation Center. They were able to scramble and get last minute airline tickets, with Elizabeth telling the Brave Festival organizers that they would forfeit the money they were to receive for performing so that they could fly the boys over. Levi was asked to give his now-famous airport lecture to the boys, and they were off on their first overseas adventure.

Emalka first reconnected with the orchestra when she popped in to see them during a rehearsal. "When I got there and entered the hall, I started to cry," Emalka said over coffee in Warsaw a few weeks after the festival. "It was so surreal, and they stopped and we hugged. It was like seeing best friends after a long time." The next day at rehearsal,

Jimek got a chance to see how much the musicians had improved since he had last seen them in February. Charity in particular had really impressed him during the jazz festival in terms of how much she had matured as a musician and a person. "She is twice the musician and twice the person in terms of confidence and in terms of being a baller," Jimek said. "In [all those] months, the most trivial things you don't think about, I have not changed, but then you look at them and they have become adults; you can totally tell, not just from the outside. She is becoming a woman, so beautiful and glamorous and at the same time, so confident, which is the coolest thing."

For their concert with Jimek, which had sold out within a few hours of the tickets going on sale and would close out the festival, the GC musicians would be accompanied by the house orchestra of Wroclaw's National Music Forum, the city's impressive music venue which had opened in 2015. For each GC musician, there was a professional Polish one sitting next to them. And just like the poster that reminded the kids every day when they walked into the GC office at Korogocho—"Music begins where the possibilities of language end"—it didn't matter that they weren't necessarily able to communicate with the musician next to them; music had its own special bond.

"At one point the concertmaster took Lamek's violin from him, and he started to clean and tune it," Emalka recalled about one rehearsal. "Lamek was watching him, and he was like a teacher. I was standing nearby and I realized I had tears in my eyes and I had to walk outside of the concert hall. And then I see Elizabeth and she was crying too, and we were both like, 'Oh my God.'"

On Wednesday, Simon M., Elvis, and Osio finally arrived after a long, tiring journey. (Elizabeth had been up most of the night as well, refusing to go to sleep until they called her to say they were boarding the plane in Doha for Warsaw.) They walked into the concert hall where GC, Jimek, and the Polish musicians were rehearsing. Jimek stopped the musicians mid-song, and everyone went up to hug and greet them. It was, said Elizabeth, a beautiful moment, like family coming home. Though the young men were exhausted, they sat down and started rehearsing.

On the day of the performance, in a venue filled with eight hundred excited festivalgoers, the director of the festival got up and told the crowd how important it was that GC had come to the festival. Elizabeth was then introduced and she gave a brief speech, including how Jimek, Manolo, and Emalka had become an important part of the GC ecosystem. The GC musicians, dressed in bright multicolored shirts in the Kenyan design vernacular, first played seven songs from their repertoire, including opening with "Safari Ya Bamba" (an arrangement specially done by Levi and Jim Pywell) and then "Oye," "Todii," and "Hapo Zamani," all pieces they had been polishing for years.

"The organizers asked us to share the music we were going to play so that they could practice and play with us," said Wamocho, who conducted the first half of their performance while Jimek played drums. "I went, 'Shit, it's [only] in our heads and hearts.' So, Erick and I had to divide up, transcribe and arrange the harmonies, and then, boom, we had sheet music to share. It made life easier. It was stressful, but it worked out in the end, and I feel we had grown and learned a few things in the process."

The second half of the show was Jimek's "Hip-Hop Orchestrated," which the crowd went crazy for. There was even a standing ovation at the end, with people crying in part because not only was it the end of the festival, but also because they were so moved by the performance they had just seen. It was incredibly poignant for not just the audiences, but for the musicians and all those involved in getting the Kenyan musicians to Poland. "People were crying, really," said Emalka. "And I saw Krzysztof Materna, one of Poland's biggest producers, actors, and directors, crying. He was crying so hard."

For Chris Szymczak, the person who originally told Jimek about Ghetto Classics and had come from New York for the festival, it felt like things had come full circle. "We brought it home in some way," he said. "We had cried so much in Nairobi when we were there the first time. But for this concert, I can say I was at peace. I saw them on their first trip abroad and it was crazy. It showed me that literally everything is possible."

Charity agreed, saying that the whole experience was a game changer for her. "Poland made me think hard about my life," she said, "and I realized that it all starts with me."

Twelve

A year and a half after their dazzling debut in Poland, Kamau, Teddy, Charity, Tracy, Simon M., Lewinsky, and several other GC members were packing up their instruments after a three-hour-long Saturday rehearsal. It was January 2020, and the GC members were in Lausanne, Switzerland, to perform in a concert the next day alongside members of the Conservatory's orchestra, as well as with six teenage girls from Jorge's Fundación Crescendo con la Musica program in Mexico. The 2020 Youth Olympic Games were being held in and around the glistening blue waters of Lake Geneva, and Jorge figured that could be a great platform to show off some of the great musical partnerships happening between Kenya, Mexico, and Switzerland.

So, when Jorge and Elizabeth suddenly called Kamau over to the side of the stage, he looked perplexed as to why he was being singled out as everyone else was milling around ready to go explore more of Lausanne. The gangly teenager had now filled out into a tall young man, his four-inch dreadlocks now flecked with blonde bits, but his charmingly quirky mannerisms still remained. Sporting a baby blue T-shirt and green camouflage trousers, he headed over to the piano to see what Jorge wanted just as Elizabeth came around from the other side holding a large, hard, black cello case. Kamau was being presented with his own cello, donated by the first cellist of the Geneva-based Orchestre de la Suisse Romande.

Kamau was not one to betray his emotions, but it was obvious to everyone that he was flabbergasted. He covered his face in his hands and took a few steps backwards and momentarily turned his back to Jorge, trying to compose himself. As Jorge went to open up the case, and Levi and Elizabeth shushed a lone trumpet player who was still practicing, Kamau, beaming as he moved hands back and forth over his dreadlocks, came back over to check out his new instrument. Jorge took it out of the case and handed it to him and Kamau placed his right hand to his chest in a heartfelt gesture. He gave Jorge a huge hug. A few seconds later, with Levi filming a video of the presentation and other GC members coming over to see what the commotion was all about, Kamau couldn't stop moving around, putting one hand over his mouth while the other hand tightly grasped the neck of the large honey-hued instrument. It almost looked like he was strangling it and would never let go.

Getting his own instrument was huge for Kamau because up until this point he'd always played borrowed cellos, as GC only had four in their possession. He'd said eighteen months before in East Hampton that he wanted to be a soil scientist, but had given up on that idea a year earlier when he found out that he did not score well enough on his secondary school final exams to get into a university at that time. Since then he had been making ends meet by tutoring young musicians in GC programs at St. John's and in Mukuru Kwa Ruben, and he also played with some of the older members of the GC orchestra at events across Nairobi, where they were paid small fees for their professional musical services.

But he still had big dreams of furthering his musical education and so while in Lausanne, he had sent an audition video—performing part of Elgar's "Cello Concerto"—to Berlin's Barenboim-Said Akademie, where he hoped to get a scholarship for their artist diploma program. This cello meant not only that now he could practice his beloved instrument whenever he wanted, but also having his own cello would allow him to pursue his livelihood unencumbered by circumstantial constraints.

* * *

Over the last eighteen months since the members' international premiere, a number of momentous events had happened in the overall life of Ghetto Classics, which had led it down a path to a pivotal crossroads as an organization. The most agonizing and impactful of those events had been the death of Bob Collymore in July 2019.

The Safaricom CEO had been battling leukemia for a few years, and in April 2019 it was announced that he would be stepping down from the helm of the company, effective in August. (He had been on sick leave at that point for several months.) Elizabeth was not only deeply worried about her friend's health, of course, but she was also concerned about what his departure would mean for Safaricom's support for GC, which had been a major boost for the organization for the last five years and something Bob had initiated through the Safaricom Jazz Festival. Elizabeth had talked at length about what all the possible financial scenarios were for the orchestra during a luncheon in Nairobi in May 2019, where some GC members, including Kamau, were doing a gig.

Just as the dessert course was about to start, she received a text and gave out a small "whoop" at the table. Bob, it seemed, was feeling well enough to go back to work for another year (which would complete his original contract) and therefore it seemed very likely that Safaricom might sign on to support GC for another three years when their contract came up for renegotiation in March 2020. With that good news she hit up to the dessert buffet, filling her plate with chocolate mousse and delicate sponge cakes.

But only a few short weeks later he died. Shocked and devastated, Elizabeth had no idea that he had taken a turn for the worse. In fact, only a few family members and friends—including former Safaricom CEO Michael Joseph—had been aware that his death was imminent. Having not known how ill he was, Elizabeth had been somewhat perplexed by a text she received from him a few days before he died. In the message he told her how proud he was of how she and Duncan had brought his dream of the multicultural SYO to life.

He also said what a privilege it was to have witnessed firsthand the "fantastic" work she had done. "I use the word fantastic because only in fantasy can you dream of going into the most deprived communities in the world and lifting children's confidence, building skills, seeing the world, and making people cry," he wrote to her, likely referring to the time he shed tears of joy after the first GC concert with Jimek. He also said that he could never have imagined that these kids from this slum of slums would appear as guests on an album of a Grammy-winning musician. Months later, Elizabeth still got a bit emotional when talking about those last words that Bob would ever send to her. "I still can't believe he is gone," she said as she watched the glacial midwinter waters of Lake Geneva lap up onto the shore below.

It had been Grammy winner Kirk Whalum who Bob had been referencing in his last text to her. Having been one of the headlining guests at a Safaricom Jazz Festival event in 2015, the American saxophonist, who has played with everyone from Barbra Streisand to Whitney Houston, made a promise to Elizabeth that one day he would come back and record a song with the Ghetto Classics members. He fulfilled that pledge in early 2018 when he returned to Nairobi to work with the musicians on a piece for his album, *Humanité*, which was released in October 2019.

Aaron Rimbui, a Kenyan pianist and producer, had met Kirk at the festival and had sent him a song he had recorded called "Kwetu." Kirk fell in love with it and thought the song might be the perfect piece to work with the GC kids on, and so he and his British producer, James McMillan, set up a makeshift recording studio at Safaricom. "We had a seminar in how you make a sound that is acceptable to be on a record," Kirk said. "And it was so wonderful to see the kids' eyes light up. You could tell many of them were nervous, but it was a cool experience overall. We had to go in and do a little doctoring to make it work, but when you hear it you will definitely smile."

Another track was also a nod to the impact that GC and the slum had had on Kirk. Entitled "Korogocho," the song featured both Aaron Rimbui and Marcus Miller, an American jazz composer and musician who has performed with the likes of Miles Davis and Luther Vandross. (Marcus had also come to visit and jam with the musicians at St. John's while in town for the 2019 jazz fest.) "We have endeavored to remain involved in some way," Kirk said about his work with GC.

Though Bob unfortunately did not live long enough to see the album released, he did get a chance to share in the excitement at the end of 2018, when the GC members recorded a cover of Thomas Wesonga's "Tushangilie Kenya," a beloved patriotic song from the 1980s, which they released as a music video. President Kenyatta liked the song so much that he even Tweeted the video on his official Twitter page, stating that: "Ghetto Classics have distinguished themselves as one of the most talented groups in #Kenya."

That version of the song must have also struck a chord with his wife, Margaret Kenyatta, because in August 2019, she made a visit to St. John's to see the GC musicians perform, to plant a tree in the garden, and get a tour of the facilities. The first lady, who that day became an official patron of Ghetto Classics, had brought with her Kenya's minister of sports, culture, and heritage, Amina C. Mohamed, as part of her delegation to Korogocho. At first, Minister Mohamed, a lawyer and diplomat who had served as both chairwoman for the International Organization on Migration as well as deputy executive director for the United Nations Environment Programme, didn't seem moved by the tour as she was shown around with the other dignitaries.

But something must have deeply touched the stoic politician because Elizabeth noticed she went off script from the speech that she had with her, and spoke from the heart. Having grown up in modest circumstances as the daughter of Somali refugees, who both instilled in her the power and importance of education, she told the musicians, "I don't think your beginning can ever define your destiny."

* * *

Months later, Elizabeth ran into Minister Mohamed at Charles de Gaulle Airport in Paris as they both were waiting for their flight to Geneva. Elizabeth and Minister Mohamed, who was heading to Switzerland because she was being inaugurated as a new member of the International Olympics Ethics Commission, had a good catch-up and Elizabeth invited her to come to one of the rehearsals at the Lausanne Conservatory. The Kenyan politician took her up on her offer and stopped by the next morning. Elizabeth's networking abilities—even in airport lounges—was a master class.

Elizabeth admitted she was trying to get the minister to schlep back a newly donated violin as a carry-on when she flew back to Nairobi because the GC musicians were already oversubscribed with luggage and donations of other instruments. It didn't happen in the end, but Elizabeth's gumption to try and enlist a high-ranking government minister into her plans was so her.

Some of those new donations were earmarked for GC Mukuru Kwa Ruben, a program that had grown exponentially. The program at the Ruben Centre had mushroomed at this point to over 120 students. Joseph Muhindi, who had been the GC Mukuru Kwa Ruben director, had moved on, so now the program was being run entirely by GC St. John alums, including Kamau, Tracy, and Lewinsky.

Meanwhile, the Link Up program in Mombasa had also been going through some growing pains. Paul Sitnam left, and Celine had run the program for several months until a more permanent head, also a GC St. John's alum, was hired full time. Link Up was still in the same schools, but there was talk of expanding the program, in part because two Swiss ladies from Lausanne were interested in making donations.

One of those ladies, a well-coiffed middle-aged woman who gave off a sophisticated and cultured vibe, had hosted Kepher for three months in 2018 when he studied at Geneva University of Music. According to Jorge, Kepher's time at the conservatory had been fruitful, though he was still bitter about GC, and once back permanently in Nairobi, he continued ignoring his GC bandmates and friends.

Kevin was one of those friends ghosted by Kepher. The two men had grown up together and had been good friends. So, when they ran into each other at Rosslyn Academy, a private international school in Nairobi in February 2019, Kevin of course said hello. He was there for a meeting to talk with the music director about instruments and Kepher was there as well on other business. But Kepher completely ignored him.

Visiting Kevin in Hamburg a few months later in June 2019, it was obvious that he was hurt and that snub was still raw. Kevin had been in Germany since March, training with Michael Danner, the jovial owner of Brasserie Hamburg, a musical instrument repair shop and retailer of trumpets, saxophones, and trombones. Kevin always knew he was not cut out for a university, but his dream had long been to learn how to fix instruments. He had seen a musical market worth cornering in Nairobi, and he had told his wishes to Elizabeth and Stephanie Schiller, who lived in Hamburg. He'd been patient, trying to first convince his mother to give him back his birth certificate, which she had hidden from him, and then once she relented, he had waited for over a year to get his passport and the visa.

Stephanie had helped set him up as an apprentice with Michael. Though she did not personally know Michael, she'd gone into his shop one day to ask if he might be willing to, as Michael told me, "take on a young man from Africa" to train how to fix brass, wind, and strings instruments. When he asked where on the vast continent he hailed from (as a musician, Michael had toured across West and East Africa in his younger days), she said he was from Kenya. Michael laughed and said he would be interested, in part because his wife was also Kenyan.

Michael had been a bit skeptical of taking someone on, knowing it could sometimes prove to be a time suck for a small business. But within the first few days of Kevin's apprenticeship, he realized the young man was not only serious about learning, but also had a flair for it. Kevin stayed there for a few weeks and then had been sent for a month to learn how to repair strings somewhere else in Hamburg. He then come back to do two more months with Michael and his staff. "This guy is really smart," Michael said, reaching for a sweet, iced pastry. "He is absolutely talented, and I get the feeling Kevin really wants this." Kevin smiled, covering his head in his hands and pulling his tan baseball cap over his eyes in mock embarrassment. "He's like my fourth kid," Michael said laughing. "And he sure does eat a lot of meat." Kevin admitted he had grown a fondness for schnitzels and sausages, and his scarred cheeks seemed much fuller since arriving in Germany. Kevin's plan when he returned home was to start networking with musicians, music teachers, and conductors to build up his clientele, and Michael and he had come up with a name for the company as well: Kobara Music.

Later that afternoon, grabbing a seat in a touristy pizza dive along the water, watching both the commuter boats and the big tankers come in and out of the harbor, Kevin waxed lyrical on Ghetto Classics and the characters who had become part of his extended musical family. In terms of Kepher, while he wouldn't quite admit he was hurt by Kepher ignoring him, he did say he was angry to see how Elizabeth had been cast aside by someone she had helped to nurture along the way. "I want to tell people, 'Do not forget who you are,'" he said, referring to Kepher and others who he felt had started to take their GC experiences for granted. He then quoted lyrics from "The Way It Is," a reggae song by Lucky Dube:

> *It's so funny, we don't talk anymore.*
> *Be good to the people on your way up the ladder,*
> *'Cause you'll need them on your way down.*

He also talked about Samwel, who had first introduced Kevin to GC all those years before. He had all but disappeared from the lives of most of the musicians, except for Kevin, who he would try to hit up for money sometimes. There had been a rumor that he was still scavenging in the dump, something Kevin said was not true, but he did say that Samwel was not making the most of an opportunity given to him by his godfather, who owned a car repair shop and had hired him as a mechanic. Precious, meanwhile, had come back into the fold after giving birth to a second son. She asked the team at GC if there was any work she could do, and so they hired her to do some cleaning.

She made a pittance, but it was something. Elizabeth hired her back on as a test. "But she has been the most faithful worker; she comes in every day, and when she can't make it, she calls," Elizabeth said. "But I am trying to keep her at arm's length." Kevin agreed that Precious had a tendency to be liberal with the truth, but that she had also been given a bad rap by lots of the GC members, in part because they felt she had taken advantage of Elizabeth's nature to believe the best in people.

Watching seagulls dive-bomb the harbor in the rain, Kevin talked about how many other members have become role models and mentors in their neighborhoods, which also affects change both directly and indirectly. "All the neighbors around and the community see me and what I do," Kevin told me. "And they think, 'This person is going somewhere; he has gone from [that] path to [this] path.' And they are proud." Seeing changes like that creates tiny ripples in communities that spread, grow, shift, and transform.

Kevin also felt it was cool that several of the GC members like Martha and Kamau were now making money from their music. He also fervently believed that it was time for some of the older musicians to start being more proactive and empowered when it came to things like their education. Why couldn't some of the more talented kids who wanted money for either their secondary school fees or for university tuition organize either concerts for themselves or hold a group show for sponsors where the money would go directly to them? "They can't rely on GC for these things after a time," he said, sitting back and watching a group of tourists walking with their umbrellas.

* * *

In Lausanne all those months later, Levi agreed with Kevin's assessment that GC members needed to become more proactive in their own narratives. He felt that the newer generations coming up through the ranks were taking on more responsibility and initiative than previous generations. He also felt that this third generation was also already at a higher degree of musicianship because the structures were now in place and there was a natural built-in progression that they could reach towards. "Ghetto Classics musicians will be, no doubt, the leading musicians of East and Central Africa," he said as he sat in the auditorium watching as the young musicians started to warm up and the audience took their seats.

After the concert, where the mostly Swiss crowd boisterously applauded the performance, there was a distinct buzz among the GC musicians as they headed towards their Airbnb for pizza and brownies in the cool Swiss midwinter air. Teddy talked of wanting to apply for a scholarship to Juilliard, while Kamau was hopeful that his audition video would be liked by the admissions staff at Barenboim-Said Akademie.

Once back at the flat they were staying in, where a few days before the musicians had accidentally burned—twice—the laminate countertop by putting steaming hot pans of rice on it (with Levi having to explain to them that it wasn't wood like they were used to back home, and it could melt), everyone was in a merry mood. Tracy, still shy but with some quirky edginess, and Beti Kyalo, a very charismatic and funny trumpeter, tried with great panache to teach some Sheng slang to their bemused Swiss hosts, while other GC members and the Mexican singers did friendly battle over who would control the iPod player.

As Charity, with some serious swagger, and others got up to dance to "Desposito"—they couldn't communicate much with the Mexican singers because of language barrier, but it didn't stop the girls from trying to teach the GC members some Latin line dancing—Simon M. sat in the corner chilling out and listening to his headphones. A big fan of chocolate, Simon M. was in heaven in Lausanne, saying that "everywhere" they went, they were given chocolate. He'd loved walking around the old town, visiting the medieval cathedral and riding around on the city's metro system. He admitted he liked Switzerland better than Poland, but was disappointed that since it was a mild winter, there was no snow. "But we did see the snow when we flew in," he said, with his token gracious smile.

He'd had a busy few months, sitting for his final exams for secondary school and starting to do some trombone tutoring. Just before he'd arrived in Lausanne, he'd found out that he had received the top grades in his class and did the second best in his entire school. "I still want to study medicine in university, and my mother is really proud," he said, putting his hand over his heart. In fact, all the other young men at his school who were involved with GC, including Teddy and his twin Lamek, had done really well on their exams. "I am about to graduate out of the SYO, but will stay on in KNYO and maybe even join the Nairobi Orchestra," Simon M. added, saying he was applying to University of Nairobi and would hear in May if he was accepted. That a young man who had no father, a mother who made do by working in the dump, and who only a few years ago had no real prospects for a future, had graduated at the top of his class, and was likely to go on to study medicine and be in the Nairobi Orchestra, spoke volumes about how Ghetto Classics was a powerful conduit for young people to shape and change their lives.

Levi sat down not far from Simon M., and over a slice of pizza he pontificated on how far the orchestra had come since those early days. "We played for the pope, we have played for presidents; that's all very impressive," he said. "It is beyond what we would have dreamed in terms of the scope that it got, the publicity that it got in all these years. But we have not gone as far as we could have with the educational structure and the musical structure. Lots of people benefit from music, with very few actually playing for the pope. For all those that never will, the benefits are still real."

The goal, Levi said, is being invited to participate in concerts not because they are from the slum, but because they are the best musicians—who just happen to be from Korogocho. "So, every time you go out, people are like, 'Wow, they are Ghetto Classics, but actually they are really good,'" he said. "That is the dream."

Epilogue

Since its founding in 2008, Ghetto Classics has gone from fourteen skeptical kids learning how to sing a few classical and jazz numbers to being an organization that employs over twenty full- and part-time staff. The program has educated over two thousand children across Nairobi and Mombasa in basic music education and theory. As of January 2017—the date of the most recent numbers GC had in their strategic planning report—more than thirty GC children and young adults had completed tertiary education programs, including advanced classical music programs, while twenty former members (a number of who were part of that group of thirty) were gainfully employed, with some earning the majority of their income through their musical knowledge and experience.

By no means is Ghetto Classics a perfect or controversial-free organization; no nonprofit or development program is, no matter their best intentions. GC was a music program that had morphed both accidentally and organically into a social program that helped keep kids off the streets and out of the dumps, run by people who had lots of experience with music but not much in development. As journalist Jeffrey Gettleman wrote in his book *Love, Africa*, development programs need to have strategy, not heart. In a sense, that hurt GC initially and mistakes were made. But blunders are also made by nonprofit organizations that have dozens of development PhDs on staff. GC's growing pains, in many ways, were unique and also bog standard as start-up nonprofits go.

Luckily for Elizabeth, over the years she had people like Simon K. and Kevin, who were part of and understood the local context of the community, which is the key to survival for any development program. The thinking in the development world has evolved over the years from one where organizations brought their knowledge and resources to communities like some kind of oft-misguided gift to one where communities themselves were seen as holding the key to changing things from the inside. As Molly Melching, the American founder of the Senegalese NGO Tostan, told me once about development: "[It is about] understanding that it is not about saving people, [but] recognizing that people have this great potential, and you have potential and you are learning too. It is a reciprocal process."

I would argue that Ghetto Classics has been a conduit bringing change within the greater Korogocho community, and it has become part of the rich fabric of the slum. A generation of children have been given access to the world of music education and the benefits that it entails. While it is speculative to say that because of GC, a majority of the musicians who stayed in the program for more than three months—the length of time it takes to complete the recorder part of the program—didn't get involved in crime, work in the dumps, get pregnant, or become addicts, there is anecdotal evidence that points to that being the case for a number of kids. (Meanwhile, people like Precious and Samwel proved that some GC alums have slid back into the negatives within the community.) However, there just simply are not comparative statistics that exist at the moment to prove this outright. Maybe over time, as a way to better understand Ghetto Classics's role in the community and as a way to show how the program has created wider change in Korogocho, the Art of Music Foundation could find funding for that kind of integral research.

Getting better grades and concentrating more in class were two of the many pervasive benefits espoused by thousands of students, teachers, conductors, and music educators from Nairobi to Nashville who are involved in El Sistema-inspired music education programs, which target youth in some of the world's poorest and most disadvantaged communities. Having adopted the motto "Music for social change," El Sistema founders watched as Sistema-inspired programs began springing up across South America. When the Simón Bolívar Symphony Orchestra in 2007—conducted by El Sistema alum Gustavo Dudamel, who had just been named the music director of the

Los Angeles Philharmonic—wowed audiences at the BBC Proms, the video of that performance became a viral hit.

However, considering the proliferation of programs in the last decade—by 2017, there were an estimated four hundred Sistema-inspired projects, and one million participants globally—there has been very little substantial research to back up these touted claims. There, too, has been a concern that many programs that were started by well-intentioned dynamic leaders just like Elizabeth have failed, as often there was not a well-placed line of succession and infrastructure in place for a program to remain sustainable in the long term. Karis, who along with Levi had been a teacher in the early days of GC, left Kenya to do research into Sistema-inspired programs in the US, came to the conclusion that a number of those programs died because they were founded by musicians who had little, if any, experience in development, networking, or management. (She later went on to found El Sistema Kenya, a school violin program in the northwest Nairobi slum of Kawangare.)

Also, very few programs had a practical plan or the capacity in their administrative, structural, and strategic planning to develop and execute a long-term viable program. Since its founding, Elizabeth had gone over in her mind what exactly the aims of Ghetto Classics were. Was it a music education program with a development side, or social programs with a musical focus? (Around the time of the September 2016 concert, she said, "I want to build children, not musicians," but by 2018 she had changed her mind, saying that GC should be more focused as a music program.) Many Sistema critics felt that if programs tended to be the former, the musical pedagogy was often old-fashioned repetition and far from revolutionary. Meanwhile, if it was the latter, there was a strong argument that these programs needed to be looked at as critically as other NGOs and social programs and held to account on everything, including statistics showing growth and improvement in young people's lives.

"El Sistema proponents have had a rhetorical problem in the last [decade] in which they vastly overpromised, and, as a consequence, they tremendously under-delivered," Jonathan Govias, currently the conductor of the Iowa State University Symphony Orchestra who has written extensively on Sistema-inspired programs, told me in 2017. "So, they were saying, 'We are going to lift millions out of poverty, we are going to change the world, we are going to change the life trajectories of thousands of individuals,' [and] they have not been able to do that."

There were also accusations that a number of Sistema-inspired projects were run using the now-debunked theory of deficit thinking, where programs delivered help and aid into communities that were defined by their weaknesses versus their strengths. In other words, that it was a one-way system where Sistema programs brought benefit to the community, versus how the community itself contributed assistance, local context, and knowledge that were equally integral to projects. "In the development field, this is completely gone, deconstructed, critiqued, and thrown out the window," Geoffrey Baker, a music academic and author of *El Sistema: Orchestrating Venezuela's Youth,* told me in an interview in 2017. "Now, beneficiaries of aid are regarded as people with capacities, with the talents, with the knowledge, with culture, [and] the point of aid is for people to build their own capacities and their own skills."

Eric Booth, who visited over twenty-five Sistema programs across the globe, including Ghetto Classics, disagreed with the critique that many programs used an old-fashioned aid philosophy. "Sistema is in the intrinsic motivation business," he said. "Its job is to wake up a kid's sense of what he wants and to give him a sense of agency that aspiration is possible. And where that aspiration goes, that is where the individual voice and individual personhood comes in."

Considering how quickly and widespread Sistema programs had sprung up across the globe (though, according to Dr. Govias, that rate of growth anecdotally has slowed down starting in 2016), there wasn't much hard evidence to back up oft-publicized claims and benefits. For example, over the years it has been said that young people in Sistema-inspired programs not only see their grades improve once they join a program, but also that they get better grades compared to their non-Sistema classmates. However, an October 2017 report by Wolf Brown, an American arts and culture research consultancy, did not find that to be the case, at least in the US programs they looked into. "We found results for musical growth and socio-emotional skills writ large," Steven Holochwost, who co-authored the report, told me. "But in this particular study, we did not find kids in these programs did better than their peers academically."[6]

Many Sistema-inspired programs also simply didn't have the manpower, money, or setup to produce research and statistics on the benefits of their programs, which donors and sponsors often wanted to see in order to justify how their donations were improving communities. However, academic Angela Impey, the founder and head of the music in development master's program at London's SOAS, told me it was antiquated to try and measure the value of these types of music programs. "How do you quantify experience?" she asked rhetorically. "This is a big issue about how we translate the value and advocacy of these kinds of projects in statistical terms. You can say, 'X number of students went through the program, and X number of students managed to pass various levels of training,' and that sort of thing. You can also use anecdotal evidence, but then you are going to be taking the success stories and bias in favor. It's a tough one."

What is maybe more important is to monitor music programs like Ghetto Classics through all kinds of methods, not just through statistics. "There are a range of different ways that are more participatory than dry questionnaires that you never get people to respond

---

6　In a follow-up email in March 2022, the team at Wolf Brown explained how they did their research on that report: "We did not find academic gains for children we studied. But it is important to be clear—that was in a US context, for a specific age range, and for the specific programs that we studied. So further research would be needed to draw the conclusion that there are no academic gains from such programs. We studied upper elementary years—there could be gains in younger or older years; we simply do not know. We used the formal measures of academic achievement available to us. Those measures capture a very specific form of achievement: often school report cards and/or reading and mathematics grades. These are quite focused measures of school-defined success. They are not measures of learning (e.g. inquiry, inferential thinking, innovation, etc.). The fact that we identified socio-emotional gains for Sistema participants in areas like growth mindset indicates that those children may be gaining skills that are foundational to longer-term learning."

to, and that is one of the reasons why music projects remain marginal in international development," said Dr. Impey. "Some people do not have an imagination [for] how music can make a difference, and the actual stories of individuals. There is real evidence there, and perhaps there is something to it."

Dr. Govias, however, referred to this lack of measurement in programs as "intellectual intoxication." "It [refers] to the fact that we are decommissioning our critical faculties when we look at it, saying, 'Children. Slums. Classical music. Why are you complaining? How could you possibly criticize that?'" he said. "Every year for the last seven years I keep hearing about, 'We are starting a new evaluation, a new research study, and this time we are going to find it.' Find what? What are you going to find?"

Over my time spent with Ghetto Classics, I began to feel conflicted because I believed Dr. Govias had a point—there were very few statistics and little research-based evidence to show just how much programs like GC changed the lives of children and young people. And as a journalist, I love statistics and percentages to back up my arguments. But also over the years I had been seeing firsthand how a number of young people were benefitting from being in GC. So while those numbers that Dr. Govias and Dr. Baker would love to see didn't exist, just being at St. John's on any given Sunday could make even the biggest Sistema cynic question their critiques.

Could Ghetto Classics claim that they have saved lives? Anecdotally, certainly there were examples—from Kepher and Celine to Simon K. and Simon M.—that by becoming members of GC their lives have changed for the better. While they likely could have changed their circumstances of their own volition, being involved with a program like Ghetto Classics has certainly set them on a different trajectory. GC also has had a multiplier effect within the Korogocho community. For example, since Kevin's own school fees had been paid for by GC, the pressure was not so intense on his mother and the rest of the family. His mother did, in the end, stop brewing *chang'aa* once Kevin got his job and could pay her rent, and she went to rehab—both indirect benefits from Kevin's GC membership.

GC of course is not the only nonprofit program working to bring about change for the children in Korogocho, but it is certainly one of the largest and the most stable. Grassroots organizations started by locals also have been harbingers for change for the community, but GC has been an important part of that overall groundswell. And it has helped with community pride over the years as well; it was a huge deal for people to see their neighbors and friends performing live on television in front of the pope or President Obama, or to know someone who'd travelled to Switzerland or America, representing the place they came from. The excitement of a visit from a dignitary like Margaret Kenyatta to St. John's buzzes around the community for days on end afterwards.

GC had additionally been very lucky in having a generous corporate sponsor like Safaricom, not only in terms of supporting GC's work over the years, but also because the company had been more relaxed than a lot of companies would be when it came to things like showing growth and change through statistics and numbers. But Elizabeth, Simon K., and others know it is also slightly precarious to have all their financial eggs in one basket. After Bob Collymore's death, the jazz festival was put to bed because it cost a lot of money to organize—according to Julius Kipnge'tich about $3 million, but they only raised $200,000 in ticket sales, give or take.

In the summer of 2022, Safaricom told the Art of Music board that they would no longer be financially supporting the work of Ghetto Classics as of 2023. As of October 2022, no other large sponsor has stepped in to fill that gap, but organizations like the Borletti-Buitoni Trust have been generous with grants that have helped fund a professional training program to improve the standard and quality of music lessons for GC students. Getting a new corporate sponsor, or a few, could be beneficial as well, but most organizations not only want to document how a program is growing and changing people's lives, they also require accounting for every bob spent. As Elizabeth has said, oftentimes it's practically impossible to get receipts when she gives money to kids who are hungry.

Also, sometimes the money that was earmarked for a concert or event has ended up going for an emergency health or schooling situation. These are the practical issues for a small not-for-profit that gets pulled in many directions in a place like Korogocho.

As Martha and Emily highlighted, GC also needs to have some finite end for members, a graduation of sorts where musicians become alums and move on from the program. Certainly, a number of them have gotten jobs within GC as tutors, but others have just drifted off. For those who love music and want to still play, where can they go?

Elizabeth had, of course, created KNYO partly for this purpose, but also the orchestra scene in Nairobi has become much richer over the last decade. So, there are chances for GC alums to play for the Conservatoire orchestra, the Nairobi Orchestra, and smaller bands and ensembles.

Their music doesn't have to end just because their time with GC has. An alumni network could well be beneficial—not just to those alums, but the GC program as well. It could raise funds and awareness, help in terms of networking, and also provide general support and guidance. It could also mean alums keeping more of an official connection to GC so they could still feel involved in something that has been such an impactful part of their growth as individuals. Camfed Association, for example, is a peer network of over 207,000 mentors who have taken part in the Camfed program, which promotes girls' education in five countries across Africa. Setting up an alumni program like this could have a positive outcome for all of Ghetto Classics members, past, present and future. Simon K., who in the summer of 2022 became an Art of Music trustee (and for full disclosure, so did I, though this book had long since been finished and was in the final editing stage when I was asked to join), was charged with helping to create some kind of network.

Over the next decade, GC and the Art of Music Foundation as a whole will need to define their scope and find out what boundaries there are, literally and figuratively. Could GC, as Bob Collymore had suggested to me, spread across Kenya and even be packaged "in a box" to other parts of the continent? Yes, it could, but only with strong corporate partners, strong local partners—like the Ruben Centre in Mukuru—and having people on the ground that understand the local context. (Plus, a lot more money and staff to run it, unless the idea is to be like El Sistema and wish organizations well, but not brand it or be directly involved except through general guidance.) When

Link Up first started in Mombasa, there was a suggestion that some schools could have music lessons after class instead of during school hours. But that would have only worked for the Christian children, as many of the Muslim kids had madrassa school in the afternoons, a scheduling conflict that tutors did not come across much in Nairobi. It has been a great lesson in the vital importance of understanding a local context, a very basic principle in development.

They will have to also be better at managing expectations; for every kid that gets to go to camp in America or takes part in a European music festival, there will be dozens of others who don't. Lots of people in Korogocho saw people like Kepher, Celine, Teddy, and Kamau going off to the four corners of the globe and meeting celebrities and presidents. But they were the exceptions, not the rule; for most GC kids, the program will always just be about having a great time jamming to music on weekend afternoons, and it will be a place where they can park their troubles for a time.

Jorge is still keen to raise money to move GC out of Korogocho to somewhere away from the dump, away from the crime and the violence. On one hand, that is a wonderful idea. But on the other, it means that GC can no longer be a drop-in center where kids can pop by to see what is going on and maybe join up. Also, to move it out of Korogocho means it not only loses a connection to that community, but also in part, its identity. That important connection to the place, to the land, no matter how polluted, would change the makeup of the program forever. It could be, of course, something more like a music and arts center for young people, which could be wonderful for Nairobi overall, but it would change the remit of Ghetto Classics. A partner like Architects Without Borders could fit well for a project like this and it might be more beneficial to instead strenghten the infrastructure that already exists at St. John's, as long as the church is willing to continue to house GC.

* * *

I caught up with a number of GC members and alums during 2022—it has been over six years since I had begun following the orchestra and a number of the musicians. In October 2020, right in the midst of Covid, Simon K. moved to London to finally pursue his master's degree in music and development at SOAS. Though he initially struggled with leaving GC and Nairobi overall, he went on to complete his degree and get a distinction on his dissertation, which was an analysis of Ghetto Classics, based on his own experiences. He obtained a two-year graduate visa in the UK, and is mulling over doing a doctorate focused on the role that arts can play in community development.

Charity began her second year at a university in Szczecin, Poland, where she is studying percussion, with the help of Manolo, Emalka, and Jimek. Her Polish has far surpassed mine at this point. (I used to live in Warsaw.) On Instagram she often posts photos of herself jamming with other students, and has been invited to perform with Jimek when he is on tour. Over the years I saw Kamau's quirky use of language and mannerisms be a common thread as he kept growing taller, towards the frothy Kenyan clouds. He now teaches at GC with his new cello and also performs across Nairobi with various orchestras. He hopes to start a university program in 2023.

In October 2022, Teddy began his studies in piano at the Royal Birmingham Conservatoire, part of the University of Birmingham in the UK. He is said to be the first Kenyan ever to study piano there. (Though he always had a passing interest in piano, it was during Covid that he properly became addicted to learning the instrument. Teddy told me in London in November 2022 that he had "begged" Simon K. to give him the key to the office at St. John's so he could practice, as the buildings were closed for lockdown. Simon K., who despite being in London continues to play a mentoring role to many of the GC members including Teddy, said "there was no point letting the piano get dusty.") British pianist Cordelia Williams has helped Teddy with his journey and scholarship. He plans to go to medical school once he completes his first degree, in part to appease his parents. Meanwhile, his twin, Lamek, is studying architecture at a university in Nairobi, and there is a possibility that he might transfer to a university in the United States in 2023. In August 2022, he and four other GC violinists helped out teaching at a camp at Kinhaven Music School in Vermont. Erick

Ochieng, meanwhile, went to Los Angeles for a few weeks that same month to take part in the Dudamel Foundation's leadership conference.

Simon M. started his third year at the University of Nairobi, while Kevin now is the luthier of GC. In July 2022, he returned to Hamburg for a month to continue more training. Emily had a baby boy in June 2022 and ran in August as a candidate in local government elections. She lost. Martha, meanwhile, continues to tutor at GC and other schools. Celine, along with a GC friend, Joseph Omondi, runs Art Wobble at St. John's. The program was the brainchild of Simon K., who felt it was important for younger children from the ages of three to six—not yet eligible to join GC—to be exposed to the arts. Both Wamocho and Stephen left GC around the time of Covid—Wamocho went to Mombasa to be a veterinarian, while Stephen left to work on environmental issues.

Samwel and Precious, meanwhile, are no longer connected to Ghetto Classics and though they are periodically seen around Korogocho, no one really keeps in touch with them any longer. (Samwel from time to time will like my social media posts, but I no longer hear from Precious.)

As of the summer of 2022, Kepher is working in the music education scene in Nairobi. He continues to travel—in 2019, he was an artist in residence in Umbria, Italy, at Mahler & LeWitt Studios, and in July 2022 attended the Salzburg Global Seminar for the second time. He says his goal is to work in the arts sector in community development, especially examining, "How can arts and culture be used to mitigate the venom?" when it comes to politics and fractures within communities. Kepher admitted that he still had residual anger over how he felt he was treated over his "Malaika" composition and the drama it caused when GC was in Poland. He also shared that he had been upset that GC sometimes tried to piggyback off of his success—he had been the one to apply and find funding for trips and fellowships, but he felt that Elizabeth and GC tried to take credit for the successes and accomplishments that he himself had sought out and achieved.

He also felt that during his time at GC when he was the orchestra director, his recommendations were often dismissed. "If you've asked me what advice I would give [those who run GC], it is that they should accept and allow democracy to rule," he said. "I was music director, but I was not just that; I also helped create new approaches [for the teaching] of students. I was pushing because I thought, 'Okay, you've learned something. If you don't teach, they will accuse you of not teaching or being selfish.' But then if I do teach [my approaches] they were telling me, 'You're being proud and a megalomaniac.'" It was, he felt, an untenable catch-22, and so he explained that was why he distanced himself from the whole situation.

With the hindsight of time and a global pandemic, Kepher said he would love to be a part of the GC family again at some point, but he said he agreed with others over the need to create some kind of alumni network. "I would love one day," he said, "to come back to GC and try to build up a department focused on this."

Over the last fifteen years, Elizabeth—the music-loving former pharmacist—has learned to focus on what her strengths are and has worked to stop micromanaging, something many founders of startups find very difficult to do. It has also been difficult for the compassionate part of her personality to not get so personally involved in some of the kids' lives anymore. Like with Precious and Samwel, she has struggled to keep an arm's length and be more objective and clinical, relearning some lessons from her pharmacy training. In 2021, Elizabeth and the board of trustees mutually agreed that she would step down from her role as CEO and become executive director. The former operations manager of the Sauti Kuu Foundation (started by Auma Obama), Lucy Njoroge—who happens to be Elizabeth's sister-in-law—was appointed to the position of CEO and deals with the day-to-day running of the operation. Elizabeth oversees big-picture projects for the Art of Music Foundation.

Covid, of course, has played a significant role in all of their lives as well. "One of the many things it has shown me is how resilient my students are," Elizabeth told me. During Kenya's first lockdown, several young women, including Tracy Akinyi, started a program to each week visit a number of vulnerable and older members of the Korogocho community. Other members organized sanitation and hand-washing stations around the slums. Meanwhile, Simon K., before he left for London, helped to set up a weekly feeding program where GC members gave out flour, rice, and vegetables. They also started growing vegetables for the community in the new garden at St. John's that overlooks the now-closed Ngomongo illegal dump site. "Maybe, just maybe, some of this empowerment and activism that my students have felt during this pandemic," Elizabeth told me, "were things they had picked up aside from just their instruments."

Unlike pretty much anything else in the world, music has a universal power to form connections—from agreeing about how amazing a song is to debating the finer points of an entire musical genre. It can create a resonance deep inside people's souls, sending a simultaneous shiver through an entire audience when a harmony is reached or a crescendo crushes through a lull. Musical notes can express feelings that language simply cannot. I felt that thirty-seven years ago, when I heard the opening riffs of U2's "In the Name of Love," while Elizabeth had a strong visceral reaction to classical music when she joined her university choir in Canada. Simon M. had understood it when he heard a blast of notes from the trombone, while the cello's deep sounds moved something forever in Kamau's heart. Kepher felt a surge of energy the first time he listened to the Kenyan national anthem, while Charity felt music in her fingers and was always compelled to knock out a beat while sitting on a sofa or walking to school. With so many governments slashing their arts and cultural budgets, Ghetto Classics exemplifies a program that is more than just about learning music. It's about giving young people agency, a feeling of belonging and community where they can spread their wings and have their voices be heard.

Music is a global cultural diplomat that can unite people over the light touches of Vivaldi's "Spring," or the melancholy opening clarinet solo of "Rhapsody in Blue," or boom drum that drops in on The Cult's "She Sells Sanctuary." In a world where politicians and culture figures seem focused on highlighting our differences—that much-hyped negative talk of the "other"—music gives the world a common ground, a space for understanding where Grammy-winning saxophonists from Memphis, Mexican pianists, and Polish composers can speak the same musical language of young people from a slum on the edge of a Nairobi garbage dump. Despite all our perceived differences, tones, harmonies and refrains resonate the same the world over, and that's a truly poetic, unifying, uplifting thing.

Acknowledgments

This book wouldn't have been possible if it weren't for the support, guidance, and encouragement of Elizabeth Njoroge and the wonderful Ghetto Classics cast of characters I have been privileged to get to know working on this project. I have had so many laughs, a few tears, and lots of gossip with them all over the last six-plus years. The book may be finished but the friendships endure. A huge special thanks goes to Simon Kariuki Ndungu, who spent countless hours intellectually sparring with me over the book's details, themes, and nuances in both Nairobi and London. And a massive shout-out to all the people in the GC ecosystem, including Jorge Viladoms, Jimek, Emalka Ziabska, Levi Wataka, Eric Booth, the late Bob Collymore, and the many others who graciously gave me so much of their time and shared such lovely anecdotes.

To Marianne Gunn O'Connor, who helped guide me through many aspects of writing my first book. Thanks also to Mary Gruman, who introduced me to the people at Mission Point Press—including my intrepid editor, Tanya Muzumdar—who have helped get this book ready for the world. And a huge shoutout to Anne Bagamery, who back in 2016 commissioned me to write a story about Elizabeth for *The New York Times*.

Thanks, of course, goes to the myriad of friends who read or just patiently listened to me workshop the book in its many forms (third person, then first person, then back to third person) and gave me their (mostly) honest opinions: Bari Shaffran, Silvia Spring, Clothilde Ewing, Emily Flynn Vencat, Kit Maloney, Kristin Kirsch, Erika Dimmler, Gina Dalfalia (this book was born out of our brunch at Daylesford!), Sarah Goldsmith, Sarah (Buddha) Brown, Silvia Pavoni, Kate Hilton, Sara Latham, Debbie Berger, Jennifer Manners, Megan

Royle Carrella, Alyssa Hall Husby, Annie Walsh Norton, Kirsten Fear and Aida Sunje. (I finally finished a book!) Special thanks as well to London's Super Fantastic Book Club—Anne-Sophie Bolon, Karla Adam, Katie Pisa, Michelle Jana Chan, and Jill Martin Wrenn, who consistently checked in to see how the writing was coming along. To the Warsaw Disaster Team, Ewa Switek and Alexandra Sommer, *dzienkuje* always for *meble, farby, ślub*. Thanks as well goes to Caryn Mendoza for being my cheerleader since we were kindergarteners on the school bus. And obviously to Tracy Gatrell and Barbora Satkova for keeping this ship afloat.

To my brilliant mother, Eleanor Brownell, who somehow puts up with my moods and oftentimes has the exact same thoughts at the exact same moment that I do. You are my hero, always. To my brothers, Reb and Joe, who tirelessly read various versions of the book and encouraged me to continue when I felt like I'd lost all sense of direction and faith. And to No-No and Boo-Boo Bear, who were not even born when I started working on this book, and who inspire me every day to strive to be a better version of myself—I love you more than all the water in Lake Michigan.

Appendix One:
The History of Korogocho

In the Kikuyu language, Korogocho is loosely translated as either "jumbled confusion" or a "mix of junk," and the meaning of the name has never been lost on GC members, who all grew up in chaotic situations next to a garbage dump.

The slum's roots date back to the early 1970s, with the British only having established Nairobi less than one hundred years earlier, in 1896. The city was set up as a colonial railway camp and supply depot during the construction of the Kenya-Uganda railway that went all the way from coastal Mombasa to inland Lake Victoria.[7] The lands had historically been a watering point for the Maasai, a pastoralist tribe that stretched from what is now modern-day Kenya and Tanzania. They had named the area "Enkare Nyoirobi," which means "the place of cool waters," and it had also served as a place of trade for the Maasai and Kikuyu people.

In less than a decade after its founding, Nairobi became the colonial capital of both Kenya and East Africa, and even before independence, a massive rural-urban migration had begun. Because the city had inherited segregated urban patterns from its colonial past, the Kenyan capital post-independence quickly saw ethnic and economic ghettoization. In 1973, the government came up with an urban plan, the Nairobi Metropolitan Growth Strategy, to get a handle on the rapid urban expansion.[8] The idea was to create integrated commercial,

---

7   Rahbaran, Shadi, and Manuel Herz, *Nairobi, Kenya: Migration Shaping the City*. (Zurich: Lars Muller Publishers, 2014).
8   Ibid.

industrial, and residential metropolitan neighborhoods so that there would be less commuting into central Nairobi. But the plans were never initiated and what developed instead were inner-city settlements of high-density, single-story slum dwellings and large multi-story tenements, which mushroomed at a rampant pace.[9]

Around the time that this growth strategy was being discussed in the early 1970s, the first dwellings in what would become Korogocho sprang up. The riverbanks next to Ngomongo (which in Kikuyu means "rocks," and is one of nine villages in Korogocho today) were lime quarries, and workers, most of whom were from the Kikuyu community, who had been displaced during the colonial era and had migrated to Nairobi looking for work, began setting up temporary living structures.[10] Previous to that, the area had been acres of bush with an abundance of rabbits and antelope.

Alice Njoki Kihara could just recall the area when it was still bush.

Wearing a bright-green kerchief on her head and dressed in a dusty, pink dress with a blue, black, and white-patterned wrap tied around her tiny waist, Alice gingerly sat down on a small carpet at the entranceway of her corrugated home in a courtyard that was cheek by jowl with her neighbors. "When I moved here, there were twelve houses," she said in Swahili, with Emily translating. "And they were far away from each other." Born in 1947, Alice had moved to the area in the early 1970s to live with a sick, childless aunt. Over the decades she had witnessed firsthand how Korogocho had developed.

Around 1977, the then governor of Nairobi, Andrew Ngumba—in an attempt to both maintain law and order and create new planned developments in the hopes of urban beautification—ordered that the slums of Highridge and Grogan (both close to central Nairobi) be demolished and the residents of those slums be moved to the outskirts

---

9 Rahbaran, Shadi, and Manuel Herz, *Nairobi, Kenya: Migration Shaping the City.* (Zurich: Lars Muller Publishers, 2014).

10 Kago, Jackson Matheru, "The spatial implications of ethnic settlement patterns in Korogocho informal settlement, Nairobi" (University of Nairobi, 2009).

of the city.[11] "That was when there was an influx of people," she said, as baby chicks pecked and hopped over her coarse, bare feet.

Most of those people who were moved to Korogocho were a mix of casual laborers and hawkers who sold goods at the large Wakulima street market. The land was something of a mishmash in terms of ownership. A number of the neighborhoods in Korogocho were owned by the government, while other areas like Ngomongo, which at one point had been the site of a ballast factory leased by Kenyan Indians, was sold to a consortium of Kikuyus who paid for surveying to be done and started developing their plots in 1977.[12] To this day, Ngomongo remains the most planned and developed neighborhood of Korogocho. But it has also been a flashpoint of friction especially between Luos and Kikuyus over tenancy. A 2001 presidential directive stated the residents of Korogocho should be permanently settled on the land that they occupied. But this raised an issue of land tenure, creating tension between the structure owners and the majority of residents who were tenants.[13]

It brought to the fore who really owned what, with some structure owners claiming to have sole rights to the land, while tenants felt that the presidential directive should also include them. "People wanted to have ownership of the land," said Alice, who survived on the profits she got from selling the milk of her three goats. "They didn't want to be evicted some years later like they were in Grogan and Highridge. But there is tension because some people want to own their land and build on it, while others want the government to build them their homes."

As Korogocho developed and expanded throughout the 1980s— eventually mushrooming into Nairobi's fourth biggest slum, with a population between 150,000 and 200,000, and extending over 120 acres—so too did tensions over everything from those land rights to

---

11 *Korogocho Streetscapes: Documenting the Role and Potentials of Streets in Citywide Slum Upgrading* (UN-Habitat, 2012).

12 Kago, Jackson Matheru, "The spatial implications of ethnic settlement patterns in Korogocho informal settlement, Nairobi" (University of Nairobi, 2009).

13 Ibid.

food insecurity, crime, drugs, and ethnic tensions.[14] (Currently the ethnic makeup is forty percent Kikuyu and thirty-eight percent Luo, while Somali/Boranas and Luhyas both hover around eight percent.)[15] During the 2007-2008 post-election violence, at least three thousand people in Korogocho were affected by ongoing fighting. Evictions were more rampant in areas like Ngomongo and Grogan (named after the community that was displaced in the late 1970s), which bordered Kikuyu and Luo communities and became battle zones of conflict.[16]

"There are a lot of ethnic tensions because the different groups do not listen to each other, especially when politics is involved," Alice said, explaining that her home had been burned down three times during ethnic skirmishes and her cows all killed, which had been how she had made ends meet. "The political leaders use our differences, saying, 'This one is a Luo,' or 'This one is a Kikuyu,' and instigate violence."

About a ten-minute walk from Alice's—past a small caramel-brown creek littered with junk, including a muck-filled headless plastic doll and the soles of broken flip-flops, and past women washing large white World Food Program plastic sacks collected from the dump that were then sold in the markets to use as insulation for corrugated roofs—lived Sera Wanjiru.

Her dark, dank shack was down an alleyway off a bustling main street in Korogocho where the sounds of both reggae music and the call to prayer drowned out the boda-boda engines. Born in 1942 in the town of Forthall (now Murang'a), which was in the shadow of Mount Kenya, Sera had moved to Nairobi during the Mau Mau Uprising (also known as the Mau Mau Rebellion). She still kept her now-weathered bottle-green Kikuyu movement permit from 1958, which included her black-and-white photograph and thumbprint, and had been granted to her by the colonial British government. Sera had spent the majority of her life in Korogocho and these days she barely

---

14 Korogocho Slum Upgrading Programme (KSUP), Government of Kenya (January 15, 2009).
15 Ibid.
16 Ibid.

ever left her house. "I have a bad knee and there is too much crime," she said with clasped hands, her knuckles mangled from arthritis.

Her son, Solomon Kariuki, who was born and raised in the slum, nodded as his mother talked and said that he felt the violence was worsening. He too had raised his family here but he said if given the option he would move away from Korogocho and never come back. "Last Sunday, I saw my neighbor get stabbed with a knife over his mobile phone, and he later died," Solomon said, shaking his head. "It's because of drugs and poverty. The killer has killed so many people and everybody knows who he is, but he walks freely." A few days after the murder, Solomon invited the killer, who was an alleyway neighbor, out for a tea and had asked him to please stop stabbing people. Though known to be a drug addict, the man, now sober, said he would stop.

In Trevor Noah's book *Born a Crime*, the South African comedian wrote about this phenomenon of crime in slums:

In the hood, gangsters were your friends and neighbors. You knew them. You talked to them on the corner, saw them at parties. They were a part of your world. You knew them from before they became gangsters. It wasn't, "Hey that's a crack dealer." It was, "Oh, little Jimmy's selling crack now."

Noah went on to write that in slums, even if people were not hardcore criminals, crime was in some way or another part of daily life. There were, he wrote, degrees of it:

It's everyone from the mom buying some food that fell off the back of a truck to feed her family, all the way up to the gangs selling military-grade weapons and hardware. The hood made me realize that crime succeeds because crime does the one thing that government does not do: crime cares. Crime is grassroots. Crime looks for young kids who need support and a lifting hand. Crime offers internship programs and summer jobs and opportunities for advancement. Crime gets involved in the community. Crime does not discriminate.[17]

---

17 Noah, Trevor, *Born a Crime* (New York: Spiegel & Grau, 2016).

Solomon and his mother both agreed that crime was something that unified everyone in the slum: those in the community who fought in whatever ways they could against it, and those who actively and happily took part in it. He felt that one of the biggest problems with breaking the law in Korogocho was that young people did not want to work. "They want to be beggars," Solomon said, watching his young granddaughter, dressed in a blue-and-orange school uniform, come into the room and quietly sit down on a white plastic jerrican to wait patiently for her after-school snack.

He said that a group within his neighborhood had twice tried to get the village elders to do something about the crime, but many of them had over time resigned their positions out of fear. Each village was run by elders—as Simon M.'s father had been—who were elected by the community and charged with doing everything from settling disputes between neighbors and confirming births and deaths to working with police to maintain law and order. The elders were powerful and often controlled the running of the slum in terms of businesses and local politics.[18] Communication, Solomon felt, was key to ending many of the issues that faced the community. "It's like taking the example of marriage—if my wife and I aren't talking and she faced one direction and I faced the other, how will the marriage work?" he said, impassioned. "In family, you have communication with your spouse so you can raise your kids properly. So in the case of the village, if you do not have communication, how will God help them? You communicate your problems and you find a solution, or you will just end up hating each other."

---

18 *Korogocho Streetscapes: Documenting the Role and Potentials of Streets in Citywide Slum Upgrading* (UN-Habitat, 2012).

Appendix Two:
The History of the Dumps

The Dandora garbage dump, despite all its dangers, formed something of a backbone for the community, as did the illegal Ngomongo dump site, which St. John's backed up to. Kevin Obara often gave tours to visitors who came to visit Ghetto Classics in person. On the day he gave me a tour in May 2018, he surveyed the dump— dressed in a yellow Brazil football team warm-up jacket and red baseball cap, his front tooth capped in gold—and pointed out that the smoke rising up from below was called a boiler. As he squinted into the bright sunlight, Kevin pointed to half a dozen small, smoky fires that were burning across putrid hills and valleys as far as the eye could see. "They only started one fire, the first day they started dumping here in Ngomongo," he said, "just to finish up the rubbish."

These little fires everywhere that raged underneath the piles of plastic, paper, food, and general trash never truly went out. "As time goes by, more rubbish decomposes and blends, lots of them chemicals, and the fire starts again, so on the bigger Dandora site, there are much more fires," he added. As his boots crunched against the pebbles and dirt, he headed back towards St. John's dusty red football pitch. "If you don't know where you are going and you walk over it, you can sink down and get burned, and in many cases people who got burned died," he said. As Kevin and his GC bandmates knew all too well, accidental encounters with boilers were a leading cause of injuries, limb amputations, and death for those who scavenged.[19]

---

19 *Trash and Tragedy: The Impact of Garbage on Human Rights in Nairobi City* (Concern Worldwide, 2012).

Over dinner later that same evening, Elizabeth drew a map of the two dump sites, Dandora and Ngomongo, for me. "This is the illegal site here," she said, tapping the pen over her hasty rendition of Ngomongo, the much smaller in size of the two that abutted St. John's. "And this is the real dump site of Dandora, and all that separates them is this," she said, drawing a little river to emphasize the natural border between the two sites. She then pointed out the main entrance to the Dandora dump. "It is the worst thing you have ever seen," she said, shaking her head and rolling her eyes back. "It is like Armageddon."

Her words were no exaggeration.

Though the rains had dumped a shocking amount of water in a short period of time the night before, by the time Simon K. and I reached the entrance of the dump site on a Sunday morning in late May 2019, the water had subsided. The dirt roads that were prevalent across the slums were now barely slick with mud. The earth here was so thirsty that it had hungrily drunk up all the liquid manna the heavens had recently offered. Simon K.'s friend, introduced only as Pilato, stood in a makeshift parking lot next to a concrete church. The joyous gospel songs burst forth from long rectangular windows and ambled beautifully into the malodorous Dandora wasteland. After a few introductory pleasantries, we headed into the dump, with Simon K. periodically translating certain words and phrases. It was a bright clear day under the stunning and heartbreaking cerulean blue sky, which seemed to thickly spread on forever above us. Standing in literal and figurative crap, it seemed incongruous that under this same stunning vastness were not only the repulsions of Nairobi's garbage dump, but also the majestic dancing flow of animals migrating across the turbulent Mara River a few hours southwest from here.

Rather intriguingly, the rubbish was not the grey-and-brown mounds that it looked like from the bird's eye perspective at St. John's. Instead it was a colorful mashup of ruby-red bits of fabric, green Heineken bottles, blue plastic bags (recently banned across Kenya), chartreuse-labeled tins of beans, orange Tetra-Paks of fruit juice with red-and-white Kenya Airways stickers on them, and shiny purple streamers from someone's long forgotten birthday party. While it was certainly not pretty, it was surprising how strangely jolly the colors made the landfill.

Another interesting aspect to the dump was how much of the trash, at least in the initial part of the dump, was quite organized. Put in greyish-clear bags, the detritus had been relegated to specific areas—small foothills of plastic milk bottles and transparent grocery bags sat next to each other, while further away were organized piles of caramel cardboard boxes, black tires, and scrap metal. This had all been collected by the thousands of dump scavengers, like Simon M.'s mom, who then sold them to middlemen. These bags were then taken away to be recycled. It was pretty clear just how much the garbage dump was big business for the surrounding communities.

There was, of course, the pervasive presence of small flies throughout the dump, but it was the marabou storks that proved to be the most unsettling. There were hundreds of them and though not flying annoyingly in my face like the flies, there was something Grim Reaperesque about them. They gracefully stepped around the garbage, dipping their long grey beaks into the trash. Some of them had engorged coral-colored necks, likely due to the chemicals these large birds had been consuming since they were chicks. One man called Samwel G., who introduced himself to me as the chairman of the dump security, but who Simon K. later admitted was the head of one of the gangs who co-ran the place, popped over to say his hellos. He said, walking along the dusty path, that in parts of the dump the scavengers killed the storks, roasted their meat on open flames, and served the meat with rice for fifty Kenyan shillings. "It's not good for the health," Simon K. interjected, "and most of the people who eat the meat are drug addicts because very few people who can afford a decent meal will eat the marabou." Samwel G. then added that the dump trucks that came from the airport were always the most popular with the scavengers because they carried things like fresh yogurt, fruit, and sandwiches not consumed by passengers who flew in and out of East Africa's busiest airport.

As one of Nairobi County's garbage trucks headed past, choking out plumes of exhaust as it drove further into the acres of rubbish to offload its garbage, Samwel G.—a bald man with a round head and flat face whose protruding belly could be seen under his red polo shirt—explained how the "security" worked. Public and private garbage trucks, an estimated three hundred a day that came between 6:00 a.m. and 6:00 p.m., drove to the entrance. The drivers paid a fee to dump the rubbish to a Nairobi County official at the entrance. Once that was paid, they then also had to pay the "security" people. Up until about 2015, there were serious turf wars over who ran the dump and collected the money.

Gangs like Gaza, Waportmo, and Jeshi Ya Sparta fought to the death for control of collecting the money, and sometimes that violence spilled out into the surrounding slums as well. It became so bloody, murderous, and nasty that, according to Simon K., the gang members of the various groups finally got together to call a truce. In a democratic move, it was decided that there would be something of a rota system, so that each week a different gang would be in charge of the "security" and they would collect the money from the trucks. "We make sure that everything runs smoothly," Samwel G. said with a wide, contagious, and teasingly sly smile. "Nothing happens here without us knowing."

As the midday sun brightly beat down on us, several yellow Caterpillar trucks scooped up the garbage and moved it back away from the dirt roads within the dump. Another striking detail was just how many layers of rubbish were piled up and decomposing back into dirt, except of course those blue plastic bags that seemingly had clenched their stake in the earth forever. Samwel G. explained that the lower visible bits had been excavated over the years for the trucks to get through the labyrinth of garbage, and they probably dated back thirty years. It was like an archive of rubbish.

Close by, a marabou lunged forward on its legs before taking off. When asked if rats would be running around within the dump, Simon K., with his crooked smile, laughed heartily. "*Sawa sawa*," he said, "don't worry, they only come out at night." A few minutes later, he casually kicked something out of the path. At first, he wouldn't tell me what it was, but when pressed that maybe it was a dead rat, he answered no, pointing to the small brown goat's head he had moved out of the path. It landed near a ripped brown hemp sack with blue rotting meat inside, an orgy of flies buzzing around it. "That's all from the slaughterhouse," Samwel G. said as he avoided another goat's head and climbed up a mound that sparkled with fragments of broken wine and whiskey bottles.

Following in Simon K.'s footsteps carefully so as not to step on any rusty tins or sink into a soggy patch, we passed empty sacks that read "Coffee, Product of Kenya," broken plastic forks, hairbrushes, and red KFC boxes. Heading to the top of the surprisingly lush green, grassy hill, there was a vantage point not only of the entire dump—"Look, do you see the cows over there who are hunting for bread?" Simon K. asked, pointing in the direction of the Ngomongo dump site—but also the slums, and further away, the buildings of downtown Nairobi. One woman, maybe ten feet from Simon K. and Samwel G., dressed in a red woolen cap, a blue-and-white dress with a cheerful print of small yellow bananas and red apples, and a grubby apron, was sorting rubbish with her bare hands.

She looked strikingly like Simon M.'s mother.

The Dandora dump site had been around since about 1975, and presumably the authorities within the Nairobi local government figured that the abandoned limestone pit was far enough away and deserted enough to be a good locale for all of the city's rubbish. But as Nairobi grew and pushed out its boundaries swelling with people and slums, the dump site started bumping up to the neighborhoods that were nearby. By 2002, the dump site was declared full but waste still continued to be dumped there, servicing all of Nairobi's 3.5 million inhabitants.[20] The rubbish was deposited there daily and over the years it had polluted the water, soil, and air, directly affecting hundreds of thousands of residents who lived in the settlements of Korogocho, Lucky Summer, Dandora, and Baba Ndogo. As Concern Worldwide's 2012 report "Trash and Tragedy: The impact of garbage on human rights in Nairobi City" stated: "These poor communities, while contributing the least to the problem, are bearing the burden of an environmental catastrophe."

---

20 *Trash and Tragedy: The Impact of Garbage on Human Rights in Nairobi City* (Concern Worldwide, 2012).

In 2012, there were an estimated six thousand to ten thousand men, women, and children who scavenged on the site. People who worked in the dump were referred to as "Chokora" (loosely translated as "a dirty street person" in Swahili), and their role was to find and sort food and recyclable and reusable materials for resale. Though it was estimated that fifteen thousand tons of recyclable waste was produced every day in Nairobi, because the city did not have proper sorting facilities, it all was taken to the Dandora dump.[21] A report by the African Network for the Prevention and Protection of Children Against Child Abuse and Neglect (ANPPCAN) found that of those estimated thousands who worked in the dump site, over fifty-five percent were children under the age of eighteen, with some as young as ten.[22]

Nearly ninety-five percent of those children worked to supplement their families' paltry incomes, with seventy-five percent scavenging specifically for food. (Many of the children and young people also enhanced their income through drugs, prostitution, and other crimes like gunrunning.) Meanwhile an estimated seventy percent of young people and children who worked at the dump site had experienced various forms of abuse at the hands of gangs or their peers. Scavenging was dangerous work because of everything from the toxic boilers to accidents like scrap metal being thrown or stepped over. Respiratory infections were also a major concern: one of the local hospitals reported that from 2009 to 2011, they had treated nine thousand cases annually. An estimated fifty-three percent of children and young people who worked in the dump had developed respiratory tract infections, asthma, and coughs, and more than half the children who lived around the dump site had blood levels that indicated exposure to high levels of lead.[23]

People absorbed PCBs and dioxins through inhalation, absorption, and ingestion, and those elements have been shown to cause everything from low IQ scores and digestive issues to leukemia and other

21 *Trash and Tragedy: The Impact of Garbage on Human Rights in Nairobi City* (Concern Worldwide, 2012).
22 Ibid.
23 Ibid.

cancers. People who lived around Korogocho and the other slums that surrounded the dump site reported everything from decreased fertility, birth defects, premature births and low birth weight, to kidney problems and hypertension. According to Beth Gardiner, a journalist and author of *Choked: Life and Breath in the Age of Air Pollution*, over the last two decades, knowledge had really advanced on not only the impact of air pollution but also the variety of the impact of air pollution. "The vulnerability of air pollution is much higher at the beginning of life and at the end of life," she said in an interview. "And with kids, their lungs are still growing as they are running around playing. You inhale more air when you exercise so you have more exposure, and kids who breathe bad air when they are growing up have worse lung function. Poor lung function is one of the more powerful predictions of life span and death."

But for all those who drudged through the heaping piles of slimy garbage to find food and something sellable, or those kids who lived near the dump and breathed in the toxins, there were also those who were benefitting greatly from the dump sites, including not only the gangs who ran the dumps but also powerful business owners who had deeply vested interests that thrived on the existing chaos.[24] Since there was no governmental control once inside the site, the gangsters were left undeterred to run things how they saw fit. And while there were plans by the Nairobi City Council in 2012 to decommission the dump and move it to an area near the airport, conflicts erupted between the council and the Kenya Airports Authority over the idea. So decommissioning ground to a halt.[25] Samwel G. said that one of the major concerns had also been that with all the marabou storks who lived off the dump, it could be dangerous for planes taking off and landing if these large birds flew into an engine.

As if the smoke and horrific sticky smell was not enough to remind GC members, visitors, teachers, dignitaries, and guest musicians how close they were to the dump, a stone's throw from the gates of

---

24 Chonghaile, Clar Ni, "Kenyan rubbish dump offers little money for much misery" (*The Guardian*, September 18, 2012).
25 Ibid.

St. John's is a black, red, and white sign with a haunting reminder of what personal tragedies happened amid the rubbish: "Home of Hope loves babies and loves life. Don't throw away your baby. We can help." According to Elizabeth, it used to be a regular occurrence to find either a dead—or alive—baby left in the dump.

Unlike Dandora, which had been open for decades, the Ngomongo dump that bordered St. John's had only been running—illegally— since 2015. At some points, the garbage spread out only twenty meters from residential areas and fifty meters away from St. John's and another school. "When they started building the new fancy Chinese-financed ring road, they were dredging up all this soil," said Elizabeth, "so the Nairobi County administrative representative supposedly allowed the contractor to bring the soil to the quarry. It had been there for decades and was a place where people would go jump off the edge to kill themselves. It was deep and it had water at the bottom."

But as the road construction trucks began using the Ngomongo quarry to dump their waste, the garbage trucks started dumping there too. Simon K. had told Elizabeth a story that once those trucks started chucking rubbish there, a fight ensued between the gangs that ran Dandora and the new gang trying to control the new illegal dump site at Ngomongo. "There was a fight, blood was shed, and these guys won, so they got their own dump site," said Elizabeth.

According to Kevin, the rumor was it was also for a land grab, with the idea being that once the quarry was filled up, it could be used to build more shanties and other buildings that would be rented or sold. He also said that dumping at Ngomongo was much cheaper. "If you are a rubbish collector and you want to keep some pocket money, you only have to pay the gangs one thousand Kenyan shillings to dump here, while it's 1,500 Kenyan shillings in Dandora," he added.

Ngomongo was also less controlled, so people—including young kids—would jump onto the backs of the trucks as they arrived. "You pick what you want off the vehicles and then you help get the rubbish off the vehicles," Kevin explained, pointing to the main road by St. John's just as a grey truck was pulling up, with people scrambling and shoving to get on the back. "Part of your work is to get the rubbish off the truck, but your payment is what you get in plastics." Those who couldn't fight to get to the top of the lorries and who weren't strong enough to defend themselves in order to get some space—just like the pigs, cows, rats and storks—were left to pick over the scraps.

In 2020, just before Covid changed the world, Ngomongo, the informal dump, did finally close down. Many GC members, including Stephen Ayoro and Simon K., felt the #stopdumpingdeathonus campaign had likely played a part in that closure. Even if not directly responsible, the campaign had drawn attention and consternation from the locals, who pushed for change. "I think it did help sway things," Simon K. told me in October 2022. "Our community stood up and were able to say, 'Enough.' And the fact that GC members also felt empowered enough to play a part of driving that movement shows the positive impact our music program has had on Korogocho."

These days, the dump is turning slowly back into green pasture.

Made in the USA
Columbia, SC
17 July 2023

20138860R00121